Microsoft

Microsoft® Office
Outlook® 2007 Plain & Simple

Jim Boyce

PUBLISHED BY
Microsoft Press
A Division of Microsoft Corporation
One Microsoft Way
Redmond, Washington 98052-6399

Library of Congress Control Number: 2006938198

Printed and bound in the United States of America.

2 3 4 5 6 7 8 9   QWT   2 1 0 9 8 7

Distributed in Canada by H.B. Fenn and Company Ltd.

A CIP catalogue record for this book is available from the British Library.

Microsoft Press books are available through booksellers and distributors worldwide. For further information about international editions, contact your local Microsoft Corporation office or contact Microsoft Press International directly at fax (425) 936-7329. Visit our Web site at www.microsoft.com/mspress. Send comments to mspinput@microsoft.com.

Acquisitions Editor: Juliana Aldous Atkinson
Developmental Editor: Sandra Haynes
Project Editor: Kathleen Atkins
Project Manager: Debbie Berman and Joell Smith-Borne of Abshier House
Compositor: Debbie Berman of Abshier House
Indexer: Sharon Hilgenberg of Abshier House

Body Part No. X12-65200

Contents

1

Introduction: **About This Book**   1

2

What's New in Outlook 2007   5

3

Getting Started   27

What do you think of this book? We want to hear from you!

Microsoft is interested in hearing your feedback so we can continually improve our books and learning resources for you. To participate in a brief online survey, please visit:

www.microsoft.com/learning/booksurvey/

9   Working with Tasks   157

10   Working with Notes   181

11   Using the Journal   193

12   Managing Items and Folders   201

13

Managing Your Outlook Files 219

14

Customizing Outlook 235

What do you think of this book? We want to hear from you!

Microsoft is interested in hearing your feedback so we can continually improve our books and learning resources for you. To participate in a brief online survey, please visit:

www.microsoft.com/learning/booksurvey/

Acknowledgments

I've authored and co-authored over 50 books, and each one has been a unique project. Each one has also been a group effort. I'd like to thank Juliana Aldous Atkinson and Kathleen Atkins at Microsoft Press for helping get this project off the ground and for guiding it to completion. Thanks also go to Carole McClendon with Waterside Productions for her help in developing the opportunity.

Thanks go to Joell Smith-Borne for her valuable help in fine-tuning and steering the project and for tech-editing the book for accuracy—an extremely important task for any good book. Thanks to Microsoft for creating an awesome design. I also extend thanks to the rest of the Abshier House Team, Debbie Abshier, Debbie Berman, Beverly Scherf, and Sharon Hilgenberg.

Finally, I offer my deep appreciation to my wife, Julie, who put up with me revising not one, but two Outlook 2007 books while also holding down a full-time job (yes, I finally took a day job).

1

Introduction: About This Book

If you want to get the most from your computer and your software with the least amount of time and effort—and who doesn't?—this book is for you. You'll find *Microsoft Office Outlook 2007 Plain & Simple* to be a straightforward, easy-to-read reference tool. With the premise that your computer should work for you, not you for it, this book's purpose is to help you get your work done quickly and efficiently so that you can get away from the computer and live your life.

No Computerese!

Let's face it—when there's a task you don't know how to do but need to get done in a hurry, or when you're stuck in the middle of a task and can't figure out what to do next, there's nothing more frustrating than having to read page after page of technical background material. You want the information you need—nothing more, nothing less—and you want it now! It should be easy to find and understand.

That's what this book is all about. It's written in plain English—no jargon. There's no single task in the book that takes more than a couple pages. Just look the task up in the index or the table of contents, turn to the page, and there's the information you need, laid out in an illustrated step-by-step format. You don't get bogged down by the whys and wherefores: just follow the steps and get your work done.

Occasionally, you might have to turn to another page if the procedure you're working on is accompanied by a "See Also." That's because a lot of tasks overlap, and I didn't want to keep repeating myself. I've scattered some useful Tips here and there, and thrown in a "Try This" or a "Caution" once in a while, but by and large I tried to remain true to the heart and soul of a "Plain & Simple" book, which is that the information you need should be available to you at a glance.

Useful Tasks...

Whether you use Outlook at home or on the road, I've tried to pack this book with procedures for everything I could think of that you might want to do, from the simplest tasks to some of the more esoteric ones.

...And the Easiest Way to Do Them

Another thing I tried to do in this book is find and document the easiest way to accomplish a task. Outlook often provides a multitude of methods to accomplish a single end result—which can be daunting or delightful, depending on the way you like to work. If you tend to stick with one favorite and familiar approach, I think the methods described in this book are the way to go. If you like trying out alternative techniques, go ahead! The intuitiveness of Outlook invites exploration, and you're likely to discover ways of doing things that you think are easier or that you like better than mine. If you do, that's great! It's exactly what the developers of Outlook had in mind when they provided so many alternatives.

A Quick Overview

Your computer probably came with Outlook preinstalled, but if you have to install it yourself, the Setup Wizard makes installation so simple that you won't need my help anyway. So, unlike many computer books, this one doesn't start with installation instructions and a list of system requirements.

Next you don't have to read the sections of this book in any particular order. You can jump in, get the information you need, and then close the book and keep it near your computer until the next time you need to know how to get something done. But that doesn't mean the information is scattered about with wild abandon. The book is organized so that the tasks you want to accomplish are arranged in two levels—you'll find the overall type of task you're looking for under a main section title such as "Working with Distribution Lists," "Setting Up E-mail Accounts," "Communicating with Contacts," and so on. Then, in each of those sections, smaller tasks are arranged in a loose progression from the simplest to the more complex.

Section 2 introduces Outlook, explaining how to start and exit the program, work with the Outlook program window, and use Outlook's standard set of folders. You also learn how to set up e-mail accounts, import data into Outlook from other programs, and work with items such as e-mail messages, contacts, and appointments. Information about how to get help and troubleshoot problems rounds out the section.

Sections 3 and 4 explain how to work with e-mail messages in Outlook, including addressing messages, using the address book, and working with distribution lists. Section 3 teaches you how to change and format message text to add emphasis or highlight information. You also learn how to add stationery to messages to give them a custom look. Section 3 finishes with a look at how to send files with messages, review messages you've already sent, and keep messages in the

Drafts folder until you're ready to send them. Section 4 covers several topics about receiving and reading e-mail and helps you manage, filter, and follow up on messages.

In Section 5, you learn how to work with Rich Site Summary (RSS) feeds in Outlook. Through RSS, you can subscribe to Web content like news, event listings, headlines, and other information, and receive and view that information right in Outlook—you no longer need a separate tool for working with RSS.

Keeping track of your contacts' addresses, phone numbers, and other information is one of the main uses for Outlook, and Section 6 brings you up to speed on using the Contacts folder. You learn how to add new contacts, view and change contacts, and find a particular person. The section also explains how to organize contacts, schedule meetings for a contact, and communicate with people through the Contacts folder. The section rounds out with a look at how to share contacts with others, keep track of phone calls, and associate contacts with items such as tasks.

Section 7 covers the Calendar folder and how to view your schedule, add appointments and meetings, associate files or other items with schedule items, and work with reminders. You also learn how to share your calendar, print calendars, and use the Task Pad to keep track of your tasks without leaving the Calendar folder.

Section 8 expands on Section 7's coverage of tasks and explains how to use the Tasks folder. You can assign tasks to yourself or others, associate contacts and other items with tasks, and mark tasks as complete.

Section 9 covers the Notes folder, which you can use to create electronic notes to replace those sticky notes littering your monitor and desk. The section explains how to create and edit notes, customize notes and the Notes folder, share notes with others, and print and copy notes.

Section 10 explains how to keep and view a journal, which lets you keep track of phone calls, the time you spend on documents, and other information.

Section 11 helps you start to organize the data you keep in Outlook. Here you learn to create categories and organize Outlook items with categories, create and manage folders, delete items, and automatically move items out of your regular Outlook storage file and into an archive file. Archiving keeps your Outlook data file lean while still letting you hang on to important messages.

Section 12 helps you work with and manage the files where Outlook stores your data. You learn to create new data files, import and export items in Outlook, and back up and restore your Outlook data file. You also learn how to use Outlook when you're not connected to your e-mail server.

Outlook offers a wealth of options you can use to change the way the program looks and works, and Section 13 shows you how to set options for each of the Outlook folders and item types. The section also explains how to customize Outlook's Navigation Pane, toolbars, and menus.

After you're comfortable using Outlook, turn to Section 14 to learn how to use the most common Office tools with Outlook. You can check your spelling, customize how the spelling checker works, copy and cut data between Outlook and other Office programs, and use alternate input such as speech recognition and handwriting recognition.

A Few Assumptions

I had to make a few educated guesses about you—my audience—when I started writing this book. Perhaps your computer is solely for personal use—e-mail, surfing the Internet, playing games, and so on. Perhaps your work allows you to telecommute. Or maybe you run a small home-based business. Taking all these possibilities into account, I assumed that you either use a stand-alone home computer or that you have two or more computers connected so that you could share files, a printer, and so on. I also assumed that you have an Internet connection.

Another assumption is that—initially, anyway—you use Outlook just as it came, meaning that you use the standard views and standard menus rather than custom ones, and that you use your little friend the mouse in the traditional way: that is, point and click to select an item, and then double-click to open it. If you prefer using the mouse as if you are working on a Web page—pointing to an item to select it and then opening it with a single click—you can easily do so. To switch between single-click and double-click, click My Computer and choose Options from the Tools menu. Use the Click Items As Follows controls to choose the method you prefer. However, because my working style is somewhat traditional, and because Outlook is set up to work in the traditional style, that's what is described in the procedures and graphics throughout this book.

A Final Word (or Two)

I had three goals in writing this book:

- Whatever you want to do, I want the book to help you get it done.

- I want the book to help you discover how to do things you didn't know you wanted to do.

- And, finally, if I achieve the first two goals, I'm be well on the way to the third, which is for this book to help you enjoy using Outlook. I think that's the best gift I could give you to thank you for buying the book.

I hope you have as much fun using *Microsoft Office Outlook 2007 Plain & Simple* as I've had writing it. The best way to learn is by doing, and that's how I hope you use this book.

Jump right in!

What's New in Outlook 2007

Microsoft Office Outlook 2007 includes lots of new features that improve usability and add functionality. Many of the familiar features in previous versions are improved, reworked, or fine-tuned in Outlook 2007. All of these changes combine to make Outlook 2007 a great tool for collaboration, communication, and time and information management.

A New Interface

Like the other Office applications, Outlook 2007 sports a new interface, but the differences in Outlook are not as pronounced as they are in some of the other applications, such as Word. Outlook incorporates some new interface components with improvements to its existing components for a new look and feel. Let's take a look at the biggest difference from previous versions—the ribbon.

Using the Ribbon

Unlike some of the other Office 2007 applications, the main Outlook window uses a familiar menu bar and toolbar combination to give you access to commands, options, and tools. Outlook uses the new ribbon primarily in item forms, such as the new message form.

① Open Outlook and note the standard menu bar and toolbars, similar to those in other editions of Outlook.

② Click Inbox in the Navigation Pane to open the Inbox.

③ Click New to start a new message.

④ Click in the body of the message.

⑤ Click the Bold button in the Basic Text group of the Message tab.

⑥ Type some text.

⑦ Click the Options tab.

(continued on the next page)

Tip

Outlook 2007 incorporates several improvements for collaboration and integration with SharePoint services that are not covered in this book. To learn more, see *Microsoft Outlook 2007 Inside Out* from Microsoft Press.

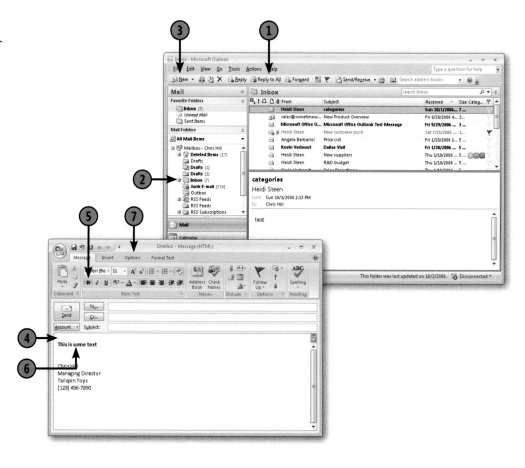

⑧ Click Show Bcc to show the Bcc field.

⑨ Click Page Color and click on a color.

⑩ Click the Office button.

⑪ Choose Close from the menu.

⑫ Click No when asked "Do you want to save changes?"

The Quick Access Toolbar is located in the ribbon next to the Office button. You can customize the Quick Access Toolbar to add the commands that you use most often, making them readily available.

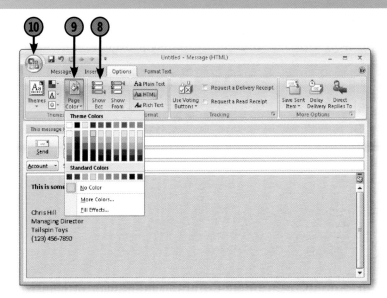

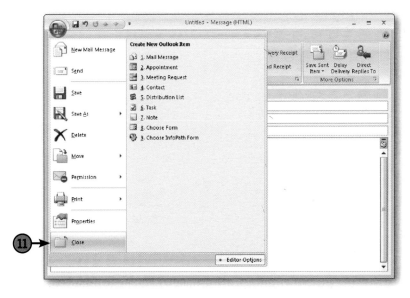

The Navigation Pane

The Navigation Pane gives you quick access to all of your Outlook folders (Inbox, Calendar, and so on) and changes depending on which folder you are using. For example, when you open the Calendar folder, the objects offered in the Navigation Pane change to reflect features available in the Calendar, such as views. A great new feature in 2007 is the capability to collapse the Navigation Pane and open it only when you need something from it. Essentially, the Navigation Pane, when collapsed, acts a little like the Windows Taskbar in auto-hide mode.

(1) Click the Calendar icon to open the Calendar folder.

(2) Click the Minimize the Navigation Pane button.

(3) Click the Contacts button to open the Contacts folder.

(continued on the next page)

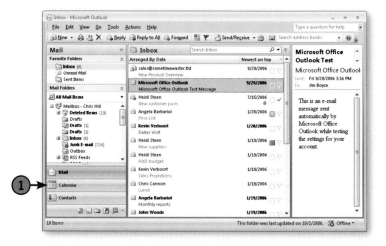

The Navigation Pane *(continued)*

④ Click the Expand the Navigation Pane button.

⑤ Click the Mail icon.

Tip

When the Navigation Pane is minimized, you can expand it for temporary use by clicking the Navigation Pane button on the minimized Navigation Pane. When you click on something outside of the Navigation Pane (such as on a message), the Navigation Pane minimizes again.

See Also

For information about the Navigation Pane see "Exploring Outlook's Folders" on page 32.

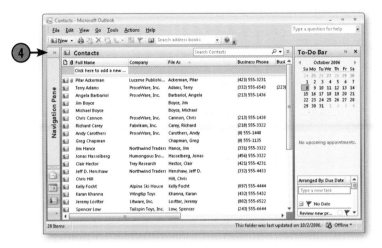

The To-Do Bar

The To-Do Bar is another new feature in Outlook 2007 that brings together information from different Outlook sources and makes that information easily available. It combines the Date Navigator, appointments for the day, and current tasks into one pane. As with the Navigation Pane, you can configure the To-Do Bar to automatically hide after you use it.

(1) Click the Mail icon to open the Inbox.

(2) Choose To-Do Bar from the View menu.

(3) Choose Normal.

(4) Click a date in the Date Navigator to switch to the Calendar folder and display the selected day.

(continued on the next page)

Tip

You can specify which items Outlook shows in the To-Do Bar. To do so, choose To-Do Bar from the View menu, then choose Options from the cascading menu.

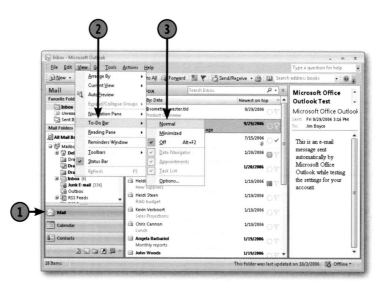

The To-Do Bar *(continued)*

5 Click the flag to mark a task as complete.

6 Click the Minimize the To-Do Bar button.

7 Click To-Do Bar to temporarily expand the To-Do Bar.

Tip

Outlook 2007 incorporates other changes in the Outlook interface. For example, the Calendar view is changed considerably. Other changes to the interface are explored in other chapters.

See Also

For information about the To-Do Bar see "Working with Outlook Items" on page 34.

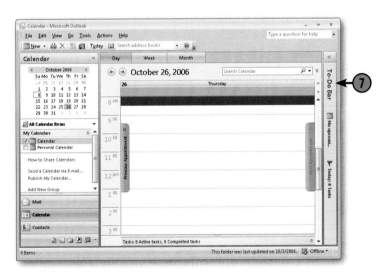

Instant Search

Outlook 2007 introduces its own Instant Search feature that will help you quickly locate items in Outlook, such as e-mail messages from specific senders. For example, in the Inbox folder, you can click in the search box, type a word or phrase, and Outlook quickly (but not quite instantly) displays the results of the search. You don't have to wait for the search to finish before you can open an item located in the search—just double-click the item to open it.

(1) Click the Mail icon to open the Inbox.

(2) Click in the search box and type a search word or phrase.

(3) Outlook immediately begins searching for and displaying the results of the search.

(4) Click the Clear Search button to clear the search results.

Instant Search *(continued)*

(5) Click in the search box and type a new word or phrase to perform another search.

(6) Click the Show Instant Search Pane Menu button.

(7) Click Recent Searches.

(8) Choose a previous search from the cascading menu to view the results of that search.

(9) Click the Show Instant Search Pane Menu button again, and choose Search Options from the cascading menu.

(10) Click Change to open a Color dialog box you can use to set the color for highlighted search words.

(11) Specify whether you want to search the current folder only or all folders.

(12) Click OK.

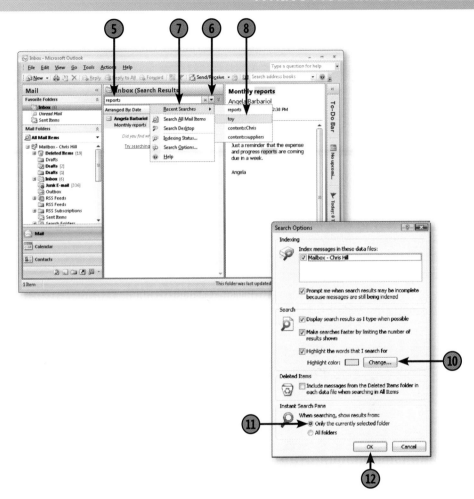

Using the Query Builder

The Query Builder lets you specify additional search parameters to locate items. The contents of the Query Builder change according to the folder in which you are working. For example, the search criteria in the Inbox are different from the criteria in the Calendar folder.

① Click the Mail button to open the Inbox.

② Click the Expand the Query Builder button to open the Query Builder.

③ Click in the Body field and type a word you want to search for in the body of the messages.

④ Outlook displays the results of the search.

⑤ Click the Add Criteria button.

(continued on the next page)

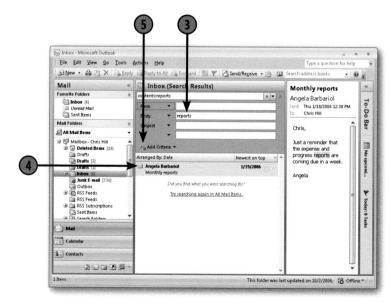

Using the Query Builder *(continued)*

6 Choose In Folder from the Add Criteria menu.

7 The In Folder field appears in the Query Builder.

8 Type the name of a folder you want to search, such as Drafts.

9 Outlook changes the results of the search based on the new criteria.

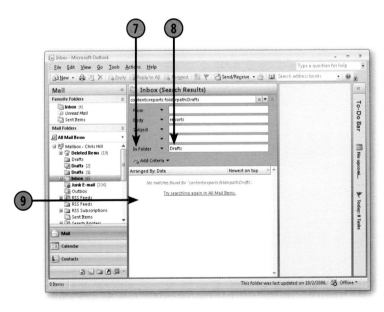

Calendar Changes

Outlook 2007 sports a new look for its Calendar folder with additional color and visual elements. The Calendar also adds a Daily Task List pane at the bottom of the window. The Daily Task List shows the tasks that are due on the current date, such as tasks with that day's due date or e-mail messages with a follow-up date of that day.

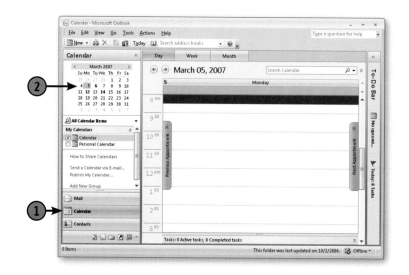

① Click the Calendar icon in the Navigation Pane to display the Calendar folder.

② Click a bolded date to view that date's appointments.

③ Click the Month tab to show the entire month.

(continued on the next page)

See Also

For information about working with tasks and the various task views see "Viewing Your Tasks" on page 158.

Tip

The appearance of the Week view is another change in the Calendar folder. No longer a two-column, day-planner view, the Week view is more like the Work Week view in previous versions.

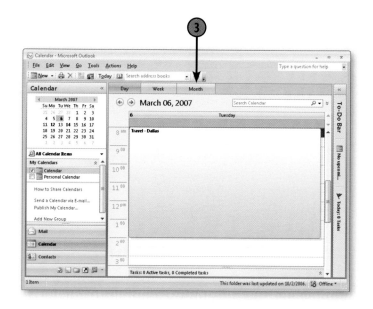

Calendar Changes *(continued)*

④ Click Medium to only show lines for appointments in the Calendar, rather than appointment subjects.

⑤ Click the Day tab to view the day only.

⑥ Click the Expand button to view the Daily Task List.

⑦ Or, choose Daily Task List from the View menu, then choose Normal.

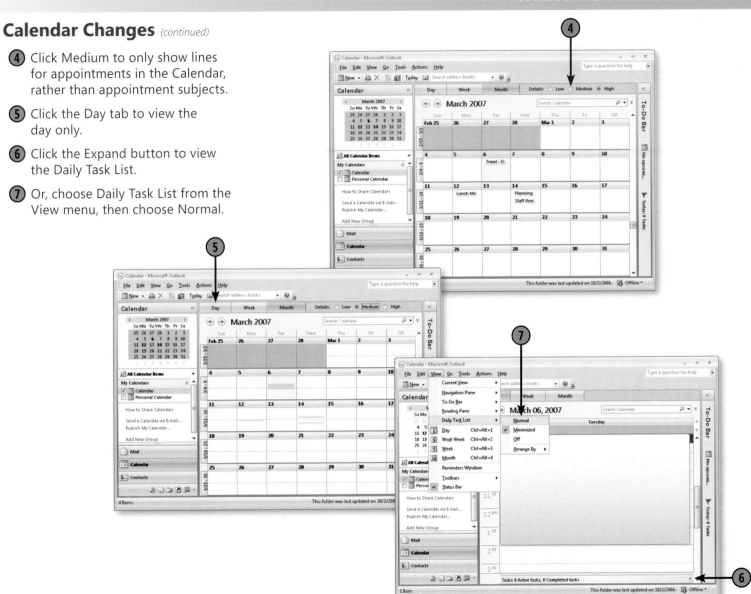

The Scheduling Assistant

The Scheduling Assistant, which is available with Exchange Server 2007 accounts, automatically reviews attendee schedules and proposes a time for a meeting. You can select a different time if needed.

1. Click the Calendar icon in the Navigation Pane to display the Calendar folder.

2. Click a date in the future.

3. Click the arrow beside the New button and choose Meeting Request from the menu.

4. Enter e-mail addresses in the To field, separated by semicolons

5. Type text into the Subject field.

6. Click Scheduling Assistant in the Show group of the ribbon's Meeting tab.

(continued on the next page)

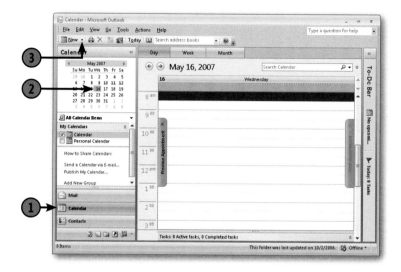

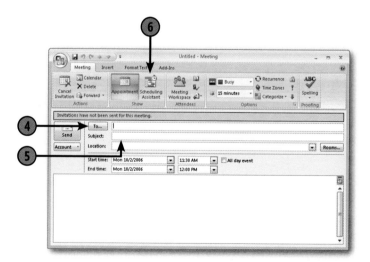

The Scheduling Assistant *(continued)*

7 Outlook automatically selects a time for the meeting based on all participants' schedules.

8 View other suggested times and select an appropriate time.

9 Click a time slot to choose that time for the meeting.

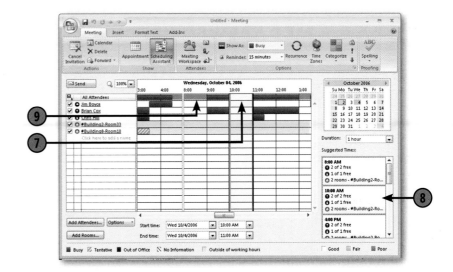

See Also

For information about scheduling meetings see "Setting Up a Meeting" on page 142.

Using Calendar Overlays

In previous versions of Outlook, you could open another Calendar folder in a new window to view the appointments in that calendar. You can still do that in Outlook 2007, but you can also view two calendars side by side. Even better, Outlook 2007 lets you overlay calendars to see a combined view. For example, you can keep a personal calendar and a work calendar, and overlay them when you need to see a combined schedule.

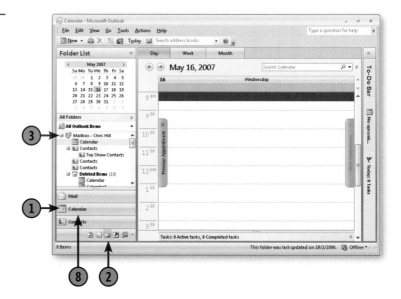

1. Click the Calendar icon in the Navigation Pane to display the Calendar folder.

2. Click the Folder List button.

3. Right-click Mailbox or Personal Folders and choose New Folder.

4. Type a name for your new calendar in the Name field.

5. Choose Calendar Items from the Folder Contains drop-down list.

6. Click OK.

(continued on the next page)

Using Calendar Overlays *(continued)*

7 Click the Calendar icon again.

8 Click Personal Calendar to view the two calendars side by side.

9 Click and add an appointment to the Personal Calendar by typing some text.

10 Click and add an appointment to the primary Calendar by typing some text.

11 Click the View in Overlay Mode button to view the calendars merged together.

12 Click the View in Side-by-Side Mode button to switch back to side-by-side mode.

13 Click the check box again to clear it and hide the Personal Calendar.

Tip

You can view more than two calendars in side-by-side or overlay mode.

See Also

For information about working with the Calendar see "Viewing Your Calendar" on page 134.

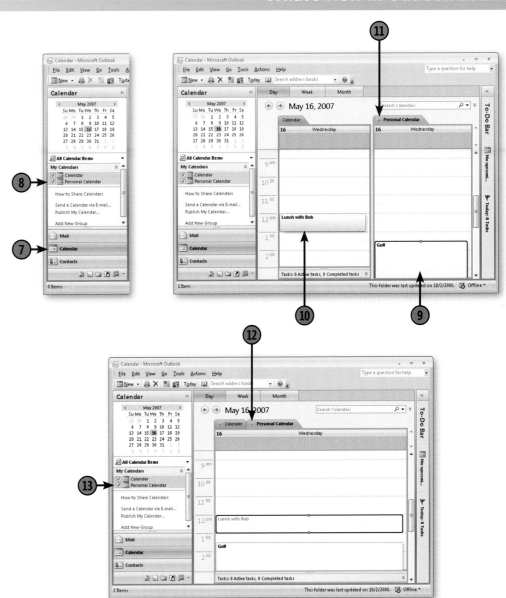

E-mail Changes

Many people spend a majority of their time working in the mail folders in Outlook. So, Microsoft has improved mail features in Outlook 2007 in a number of ways, both visual and functional.

- Outlook 2007 now can automatically set up e-mail accounts for you based on a small amount of information you provide, such as your e-mail address and name.

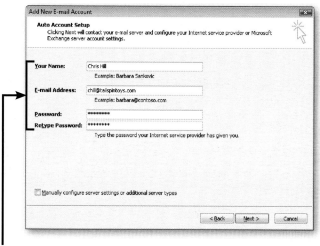

Automatically set up e-mail accounts

See Also

For information about working with e-mail see "Receiving E-mail" on page 74.

Tip

You can now schedule the Out of Office Assistant ahead of time, turning it on at the specified time. You can also specify different out-of-office messages for recipients in your organization from those outside of it. These new Out of Office features require Exchange Server 2007 on the back end.

- You can preview certain types of documents right in the Reading Pane without having to open the attachment or the message containing it.

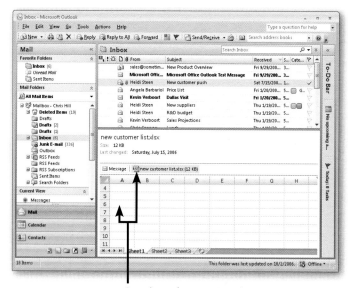

Preview documents in the Reading Pane

■ Unified Messaging, when used with Exchange Server 2007, enables you to have your voice messages and faxes delivered to your Inbox along with your e-mail.

Voice messages and faxes delivered to your Inbox

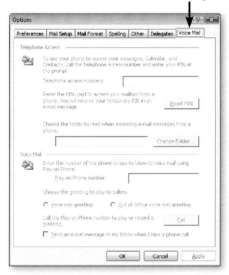

■ Outlook 2007 also adds a phishing filter to help guard against phishing attacks in which official-looking but false messages attempt to direct you to malicious sites or obtain personal information such as credit card or banking information.

Phishing Filter

Tip ✓

Another new feature is E-mail Postmarks. Outlook 2007 stamps each message with a uniquely generated electronic postmark. This helps reduce spamming by imposing a small processing load on the computer. This load is negligible when sending usual e-mail messages, but imposes an unacceptable load on spammers trying to send messages to a large number of recipients. Outlook 2007 also recognizes the postmark on messages that it receives, helping it to determine that the message is not junk mail.

Tip ✓

A new Managed Folders feature works in conjunction with Exchange Server 2007 to provide a means for archiving messages to meet legal requirements such as Sarbanes-Oxley and HIPAA, and corporate policy requirements. Managed folders look and function like other message store folders (such as the Inbox folder), but policies assigned to the managed folder determine retention and other policy-based behavior. In addition, the user cannot move, rename, or delete the managed folders. These restrictions ensure that the users cannot bypass retention policies.

Color Categories

Categories in Outlook are like tags that you associate with Outlook items (messages, appointments, and so on). In previous versions of Outlook, categories were strictly text. Outlook 2007 introduces color categories to make categories more visible and more useful. By associating a color with a category, you make it easier to quickly identify items that have a specific assigned category. This is particularly true when you are using a list view that is not grouped by category. For example, you might assign the Blue category to all e-mail messages from a certain sender. You can then tell at a glance when looking at the Inbox which messages are from that sender.

① Click the Mail icon on the Navigation Pane to open the Inbox.

② Click a message you want to categorize.

③ Click the Categorize icon on the toolbar.

④ Choose a category from the list.

⑤ Repeat steps 3 and 4 to assign additional categories as desired.

⑥ If this is the first time you have used a category, Outlook asks if you want to rename it.

⑦ Click No.

⑧ The category indicator(s) appear in the Reading Pane.

(continued on the next page)

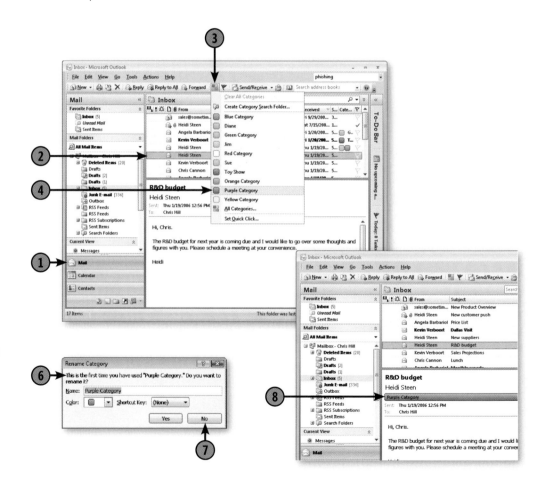

Color Categories (continued)

⑨ Click the Categorize icon on the toolbar.

⑩ Choose All Categories from the menu to show the Color Categories dialog box.

⑪ Place a check beside categories to assign those categories to the selected message.

⑫ Choose a color for the selected category if you want to change the color.

⑬ Click New to create a new category.

⑭ Type a category name.

⑮ Choose a color.

⑯ Click OK

⑰ Click OK again to close the Color Categories dialog box.

Tip

When the Reading Pane is located at the right of the Outlook window, you can assign a single, predefined quick-pick category to an item by clicking the Quick Click column in the item header. To specify the Quick Click category, choose Categorize from the Edit menu and choose Set Quick Click to open the Set Quick Click dialog box, where you can choose one category to be the Quick Click category.

See Also

For information about color categories, see "Using Categories" on page 202.

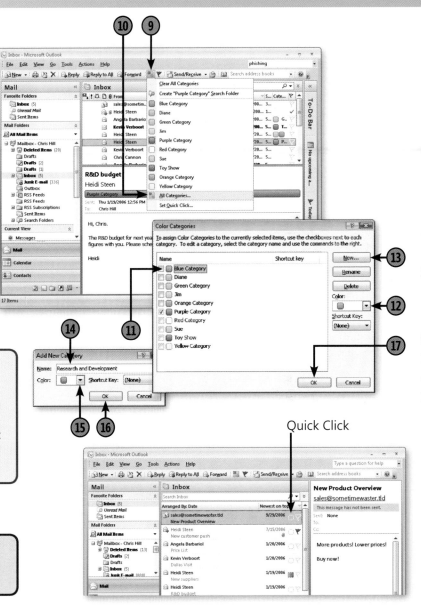

Quick Click

3

Getting Started

Microsoft Outlook is designed to help you manage almost every aspect of your day. With Outlook you can manage your e-mail, contacts, calendar, and tasks. You can even keep track of your phone calls, time spent on documents, and other tasks and events.

Even with all of the features it contains, Outlook is easy to use. The program provides simple forms for creating and viewing messages, meetings, tasks, and other items. You have several options for viewing your information in Outlook, and the program offers the ability to customize the existing views and create new ones to give you exactly the view of your data that you need. With this book in hand, you'll be up to speed with Outlook in just a few hours.

This section of the book offers a quick overview of Outlook and how to start using it. You learn how to open Outlook and how to move through the various folders it uses to store your data. You also learn how to work with Outlook items (such as messages, meetings, and contacts), import e-mail accounts and messages from other programs, and get help when you need more information on a particular feature or task.

Outlook 2007 at a Glance

Although Outlook is easy to use, the Outlook program window can seem overwhelming to new users because it contains so much information. Once you understand how Outlook organizes and presents that information, however, you'll have no trouble moving from folder to folder to view and manage your information. The main program window organizes all of your Outlook folders for easy access, and individual windows help you work with the different types of Outlook items.

Overview of Outlook Program Window

Outlook provides several folders and ways to view the contents of those folders. The default view is the Outlook Today view, which combines several types of data in one view.

Select commands from the Menu bar.

Perform common tasks with the Standard toolbar.

Move between folders with the Navigation Pane.

Use other folders in Outlook.

Tip

If you need more space to display your schedule or other data, you can collapse the Navigation Pane or hide it altogether. Click the collapsed Navigation Pane or choose from the Go menu to open a different Outlook folder.

See Also

Outlook Today is Outlook's default view, but you can choose a different view as your default view. See "Set the Startup View" on page 44 for details.

Overview of an Outlook Item Window

Each Outlook folder uses a different type of form to let you view, create, and work with items. Simply double-click an item to open its form, or click the small arrow beside the New command on the Standard toolbar and choose the type of item you want to create.

See Also

For information on customizing the Navigation Pane to add or remove icons, see "Customizing the Navigation Pane" on page 241.

① Click the arrow beside the New button to select the type of item you want to create.

② Double-click an item to open the item for viewing and editing.

③ View the opened item.

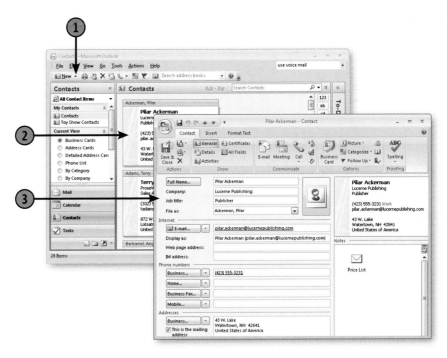

Starting and Exiting Outlook

Before you can work with your Outlook items you need to open Outlook. The program works much like any other Windows program when it comes to starting, working in, or exiting the program.

Start Outlook

① Click Start, All Programs, Microsoft Office, Microsoft Outlook 2007.

Try This!

Drag the Outlook icon from the Start menu to the desktop to give you an easy way to open Outlook from the desktop.

Tip

If you work with Outlook much of the day or every time you work on your computer, drag the Outlook icon from the Windows desktop to the Programs/Startup folder on the Start menu to create a shortcut there for Outlook. Outlook then starts when you log on to your computer.

Exit Outlook

① Choose Exit from the File menu; or

② Click the Close button.

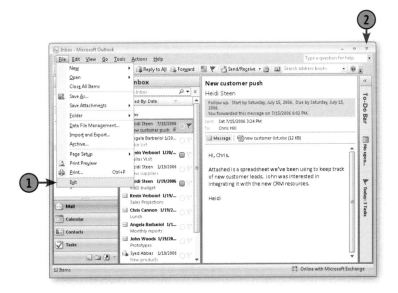

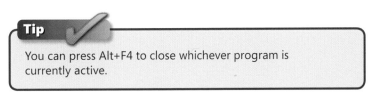

Tip

You can press Alt+F4 to close whichever program is currently active.

Exploring Outlook's Folders

Outlook includes several folders that contain different types of data. Incoming messages are placed in the Inbox, and outgoing messages are placed in the Outbox. The Drafts folder holds messages that you are working on, and the Sent Items folder keeps a copy of messages you send. You can use the Contacts folder to store contact information and the Calendar folder to store your schedule. The Navigation Pane and the Folder list give you quick access to your folders.

Using the Navigation Pane

1 Click the Mail icon to open the Inbox folder.

2 Click either Personal Folders or Mailbox (depending on the type of account you have) to open your Outlook Today folder.

3 Click other icons to open items not shown on the Navigation Pane.

Use the Folder List

① Click the Folder List button.

② Drag the resizing bar down to show more of the folder list.

③ Click a plus sign to expand a folder's listing.

④ Click a minus sign to collapse a folder's listing.

⑤ Click a folder to open it in Outlook.

⑥ Click a different icon to display that folder's contents.

Tip

You can use more than one set of personal folders at a time, and Outlook shows them all in the folder list. For example, if you have a Hotmail account, you see a set of Hotmail folders in addition to your Exchange Server mailbox or personal folders.

See Also

For information on setting up e-mail accounts for Hotmail and other e-mail services, see "Setting Up E-Mail Accounts" on page 36.

Working with Outlook Items

Outlook offers several types of items you can use to store information and send messages. These items include messages, contacts, journal entries, tasks, appointments, meetings, and notes. Outlook stores each type in a particular folder and presents the information in a way that makes the most sense for that type of data. In many situations, you can retrieve the information you need simply by opening the folder without actually opening the item.

Review Items in a Folder

① In the Navigation Pane, click the folder whose contents you want to view.

② Use the scroll bar to view additional items.

③ View the item either directly in the folder pane or in the Reading Pane.

④ In the Contacts folder, click the letter that corresponds to the first initial of other names you want to view.

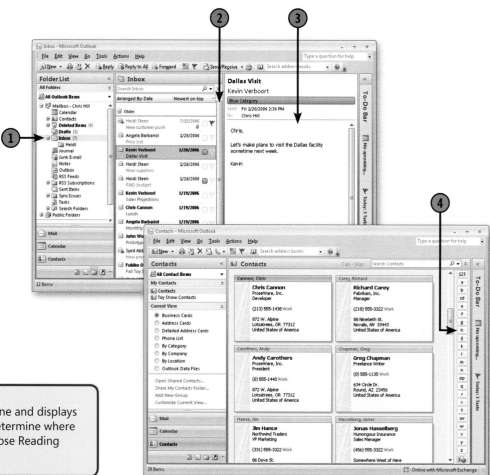

Tip

The Reading Pane appears below the folder pane and displays the contents of an item when you click it. To determine where the Reading Pane appears or to turn it off, choose Reading Pane from the View menu.

Review Items in a Folder (continued)

Open an Item

1 In the Navigation Pane, click the folder containing the item you want to open.

2 Locate the item in the folder pane, and double-click it.

3 View the item in its form, or make changes as necessary.

4 Click Save & Close to save your changes to the item and close the form.

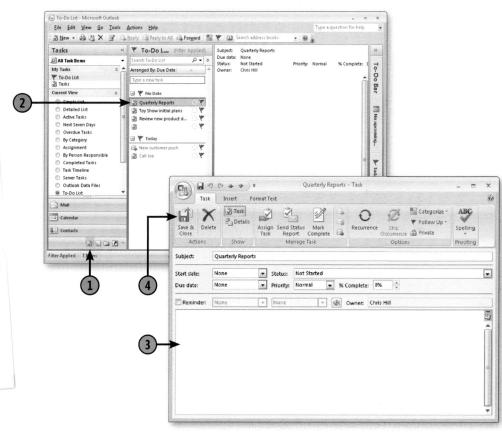

Setting Up E-Mail Accounts

You can use Outlook to send and receive messages for several different types of e-mail accounts. Outlook supports Microsoft Exchange Server, POP3 services such as a typical account from an Internet service provider (ISP), IMAP services such as CompuServe 2000, and HTTP-based e-mail services such as Hotmail. You can easily add a new account or import e-mail account settings from Microsoft Outlook Express, Windows Mail, or Eudora. (Outlook 2007 does not support import from other applications such as Netscape or Firefox.)

Importing E-Mail Accounts

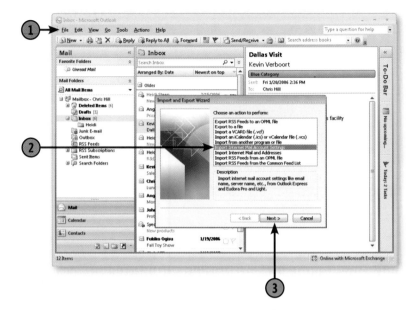

① Open Outlook, and choose Import And Export from the File menu.

② Select Import Internet Mail Account Settings.

③ Click Next.

④ Select the program from which you're importing accounts, and click Next.

⑤ Select the account you want to import, and click Next.

(continued on the next page)

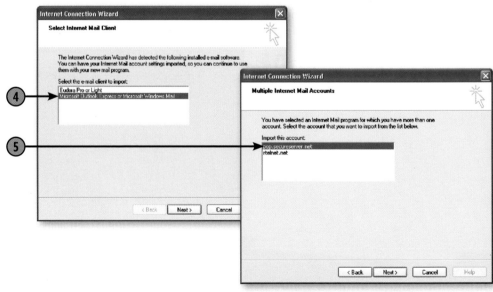

Import E-Mail Account
Settings *(continued)*

⑥ Verify or change your name in the account, and click Next.

⑦ Verify or change your e-mail address for the account, and click Next.

⑧ Verify the server type, incoming and outgoing mail server addresses, and click Next.

⑨ Verify or change the account name.

⑩ Set the password, and click Next.

⑪ Select the type of connection to use for the account, and click Next.

⑫ Click Finish.

Try This!

Entering your e-mail address on Web sites is a good way to fill your Inbox with spam, but some sites require your address when you register. One option is to set up an Internet mail address with Hotmail or one of the other providers, and use this exclusively for password verification. That way the unsolicited e-mail goes to an address that you check only occasionally.

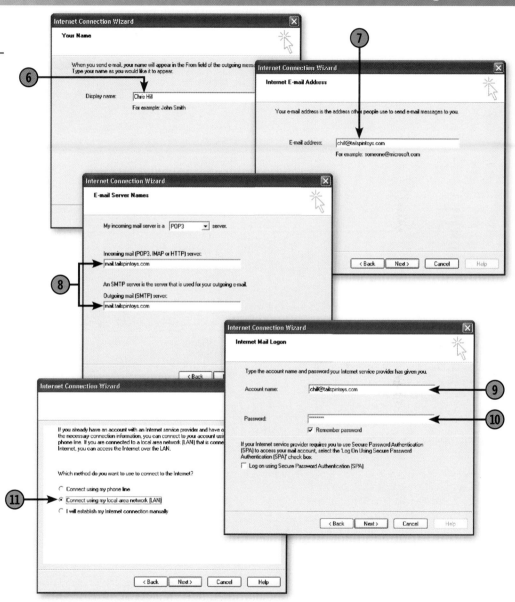

Add an E-Mail Account Manually

(1) Open Outlook, and choose Account Settings from the Tools menu.

(2) Click New.

(3) Select Microsoft Exchange, POP3, IMAP, Or HTTP.

(4) Click Next.

(continued on the next page)

Tip

You can add, change, and remove Outlook e-mail accounts, personal folders, address books, and directory services through the Mail icon in Windows Control Panel.

Try This!

Outlook can often add e-mail accounts automatically. In the Add New E-mail Account dialog box, fill in your name, e-mail address, and password, and click Next. Outlook attempts to identify the mail server based on your e-mail address and performs some tests to verify that it can send and receive using the specified server(s). If Outlook cannot determine the right settings, Outlook prompts you to enter them manually.

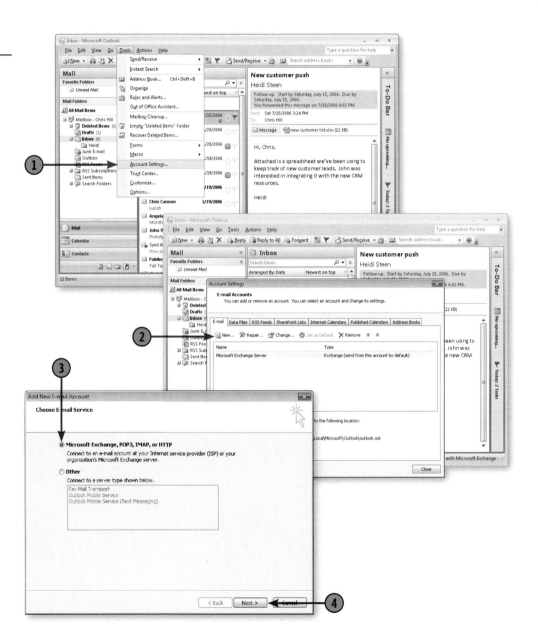

Add an E-Mail Account Manually (continued)

(5) Select Manually Configure Server Settings Or Additional Server Types, and then click Next.

(6) Select Internet E-mail, and click Next.

(7) Type your name and e-mail address.

(8) Choose the account type.

(9) Type the incoming and outgoing mail server names.

(10) Type your user name and password for the server(s).

(11) Click Test Account Settings to have Outlook test your settings, then close the test window when the test is completed successfully. Click Next and Finish to return to the Account Settings window.

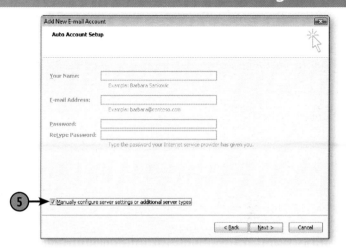

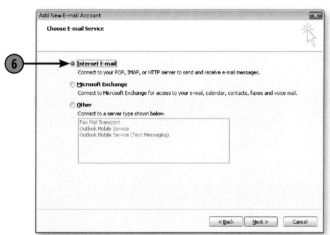

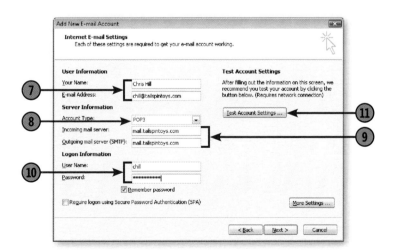

See Also

For information on keeping messages from different accounts separated from one another, see "Working with the Rules Wizard" on page 88.

Importing Data from Another Program

If you switch to Outlook from Outlook Express, Windows Mail, or Eudora, you might want to import your existing messages and contacts so that you can continue working with them.

Importing messages, addresses, and data into Outlook saves the time you'd need to re-create them manually.

Retrieve Internet Mail and Addresses

1. In Outlook, choose Import and Export from the File menu.

2. Select Import Internet Mail And Addresses.

3. Click Next.

4. Select the program from which you're importing items.

5. Select the types of items you want to import, and click Next.

6. Specify how you want Outlook to treat duplicate items, and then click Finish.

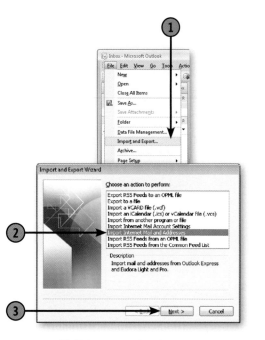

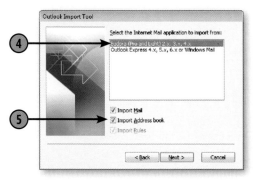

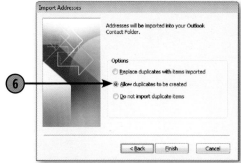

Retrieve Data from Another Program

1. In Outlook, choose Import And Export from the File menu.

(continued on the next page)

Tip

When you import data from certain programs you might need to perform some additional steps before bringing the data into Outlook. For example, you must name one or more ranges in Excel before you can import spreadsheet data into Outlook.

Retrieve Data from
Another Program *(continued)*

(2) Select Import From Another Program Or File, and click Next.

(3) Select the file type of the data you want to import.

(4) Click Next.

(5) Click Browse to locate the file, or type the file path and name in the File To Import text box.

(6) Choose how you want Outlook to treat duplicate data, and then click Next.

(7) Select the Outlook folder where you want Outlook to store the imported items, and click Next.

(8) Place a checkmark beside the item(s) you want to import. If the Map Custom Fields dialog box doesn't open, click Map Custom Fields.

(9) Click and drag an item from the From list to the To list and drop it on the Outlook field where you want the item copied. This tells Outlook where to place the incoming data. Repeat for all items to be imported, and then click OK.

(10) Click Finish when you're ready to import the data.

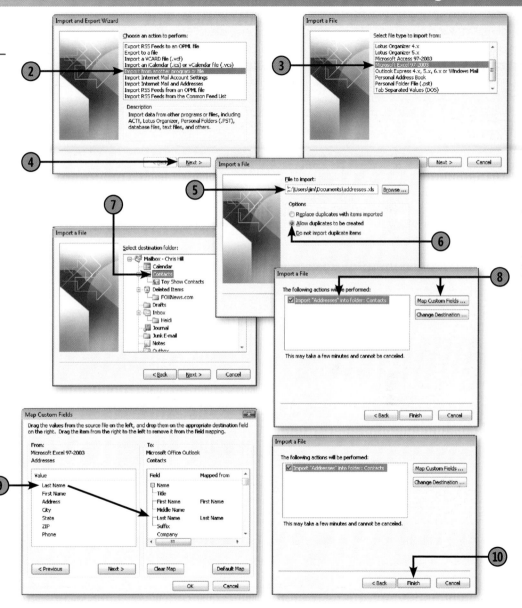

Viewing Items and Folders

Outlook offers several different views depending on the folder you open. You can use the default views to work with the data in the folder or change the view to tailor it to your needs. The Outlook Today view gives you a single place to view your pending appointments, tasks, and messages, giving you a summary of your workday or workweek. You can also use the View menu to switch easily between the available views for a particular Outlook folder.

Use the Outlook Today View

1 In Outlook, click either Personal Folders (non-Exchange Server account) or Mailbox (Exchange Server) in the Navigation Pane.

2 To open an appointment, click the appointment in the Calendar list.

3 Select the checkbox beside a task to mark it as complete.

4 Click a task to open the task.

5 Click the Inbox, Drafts, or Outbox links to open the folder and work with your messages.

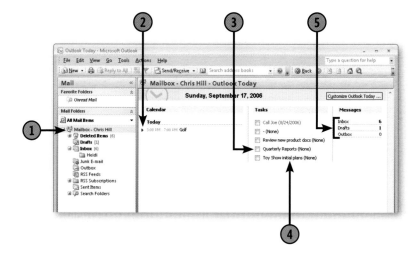

Use the Current View Menu

1 In Outlook, select the folder you want to view.

2 Choose Current View on the View menu.

3 From the submenu, choose the view you want to use...

4 or, click a view in the Navigation Pane to open that view.

Try This!

Open the Contacts folder and click New in the Standard tool-bar to create a new contact. Fill in the fields on the General page, and click Save & Close to save the contact. With the Contacts folder open, choose Current View on the View menu, then select Detailed Address Cards. Outlook displays more information in the Contacts folder. Choose Current View on the View menu, then select Phone List to change to a view that is handy for quickly locating phone numbers.

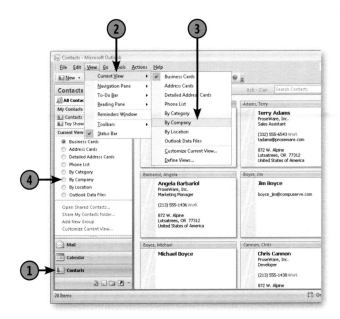

Set the Startup View

1. In Outlook, click Options in the Tools menu to display the Options dialog box.

2. Click the Other tab.

3. Click Advanced Options to show the Advanced Options dialog box.

4. Click Browse, and choose the folder you want Outlook to display when you first start the program.

5. Click OK twice to close the Advanced Options and Options dialog boxes.

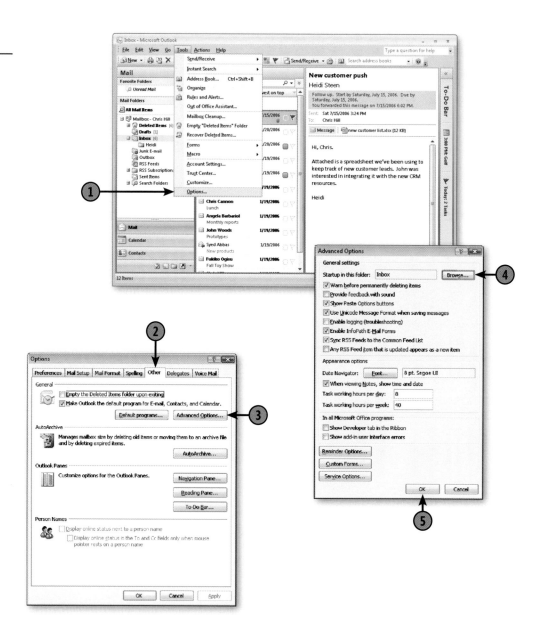

Getting Help in Outlook 2007

Every new program has a learning curve. Getting up to speed with Outlook can take some time because of the sheer number of features it offers. Even after you become comfortable using Outlook on a day-to-day basis, you'll still run into situations where you need some help with features you've never used before or those you seldom use. Outlook provides extensive help documentation though. You can access this information in a couple of ways.

Ask a Quick Question

1. At the upper-right corner of the Outlook window you find a question box. Click in the box, type a question or keywords, and press Enter.

2. Outlook presents a list of possible answers. Click the one that appears to answer your question.

Use Outlook's Help Content

1. Choose Microsoft Office Outlook Help from the Help menu, or simply press F1.

2. Click in the text box, and type a word or phrase.

3. Click the arrow beside the Search button.

4. Choose where to search for the information.

5. Click a topic heading to view related topics.

Tip

Offline Help consists of Help content installed by Setup and stored on your computer. Online Help is content available on the Internet at Microsoft's Web site. Offline Help is great when you don't want or can't connect to the Internet. Online Help is generally more extensive.

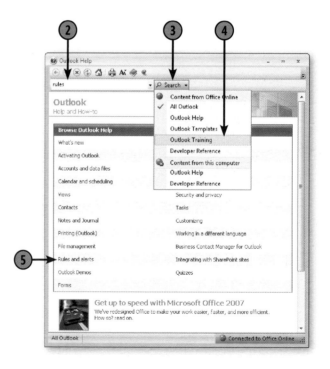

Writing and Sending E-Mail

Microsoft Office Outlook 2007 handles many daily tasks for you, such as keeping your calendar, collecting notes, and saving your contacts. But the main feature of Outlook is its electronic mail (e-mail) features. Outlook is often referred to as a universal inbox—it can send, receive, and store messages from a number of different e-mail sources. These sources can include internal networks, Internet e-mail accounts, and other sources.

Outlook's e-mail features enable you to create e-mail messages and send them to other users. With the help of the Outlook Address Book, you can quickly access a recipient's e-mail address when you are ready to address your new e-mail message. Outlook also provides ways to send one message to multiple users using distribution lists, format e-mail message text to contain rich content (such as hypertext format), use signatures at the bottom of all your outgoing messages, and create HTML stationery.

In this section, you learn how to write and modify e-mail messages, send messages, and review messages you've already sent. In addition, you learn how to use the Address Book to select recipient names, create and use distribution lists, format your messages, use signatures, send attached files, and work with HTML stationery.

Writing an E-Mail Message

When you write new messages in Outlook, you use the Message window. This window has a line for recipients (called the To line), a line for "carbon copied" recipients (the Cc line), a Subject line, and an area for the text of the message. Every new message must have at least one recipient. If you want, you can leave the Cc and Subject lines blank, but it's a good idea to give your messages a subject.

Address an E-Mail Message

1. In Outlook, click New on the Standard toolbar to display a new Message window.

2. To open the Select Names dialog box, click To.

3. Click the Address Book drop-down arrow.

4. Click the name of the address book you want to use, such as Contacts. The addresses in the selected address book appear in the box.

5. Click the name of the person to whom you want to send the new message.

6. Click To, Cc, or Bcc; Outlook copies the name to the specified message recipients list.

7. Repeat steps 5 and 6 until the message recipients list includes all the recipients you want to send the message to.

8. Click OK.

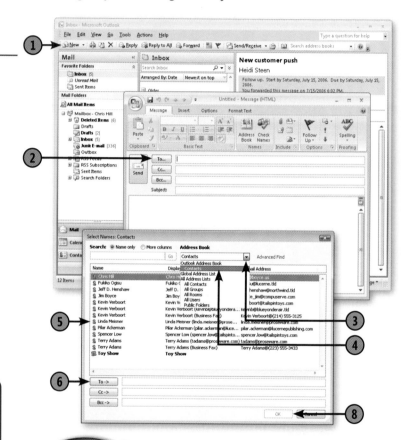

Tip

You can set up several different address books to store your e-mail recipients' contact information. For example, you might have a company-wide address book that stores addresses and contact information for all internal employees. A second address book can be set up for external contacts, such as vendors, suppliers, and customers. A third address book could store personal contact information.

See Also

For information on adding and updating contacts, see "Working with Contacts" on page 105.

Type Your Message
Subject and Text

(1) In the New Message window, type a subject for the new message in the Subject field.

(2) Press Tab or click in the message body area.

(3) Type your message.

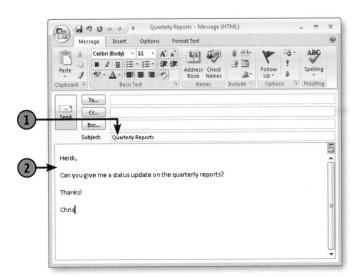

Tip

As you write your message, you do not have to press Enter at the end of each line. Keep typing and Outlook wraps the text to the next line. To create a new paragraph, press Enter. If you want each paragraph to be separated by two blank lines, press Enter twice at the end of each paragraph. This makes your messages easier to read than single-spaced messages.

See Also

After you type your message, you can send it. Sending messages is discussed later in "Sending Messages" on page 69.

Caution

You can apply special formatting to your message (see "Formatting Message Text" on page 59), but you might not want to. If you send mail to people who use a different e-mail program, they might not see the formatting that you intended. When in doubt, it's usually a good policy to keep your messages simple so nothing gets lost in the translation.

Working with the Address Book

You can use the Outlook Address Book to search for and select names, e-mail addresses, and distribution lists. When you type a recipient name in the To field of the Message window, Outlook searches the Address Book for a match. The Address Book actually gives you access to potentially several address books, including information from the Contacts folder, Microsoft Exchange Server Global Address List (if you have an Exchange Server mailbox), and Internet directory services. Depending on the way you have Outlook set up, you may have information from only one of these sources, or you may have contact information from multiple types.

Open the Address Book

1. In Outlook, choose Address Book from the Tools menu or click the Address Book button on the Standard toolbar.

2. Click the selection arrow on the Address Book drop-down list.

3. Click the address book from which you want to view addresses.

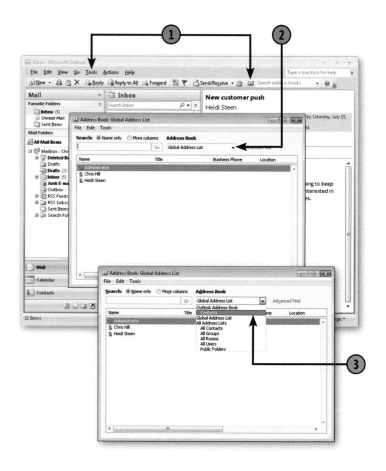

> **See Also**
>
> For more on working with your contact information, see "Working with Contacts" on page 105.

> **Tip** ✓
>
> If your installation of Outlook is not set up for other address books, such as an Exchange Server Global Address List, the only address book you can select from the drop-down list is the Outlook Contacts folder. Note that the Outlook Address Book collects together all address books, but is not an address book itself.

Find a Name in the Address Book

1 In the Address Book dialog box, click in the Search text box.

2 Type the name of the contact you want to find.

3 The first contact that matches is highlighted in the list of names.

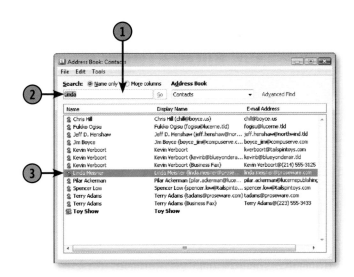

Try This!

Assume you want to find a contact whose name is Dave. You are not sure if you listed him as "Dave" or "David" in your Contacts folder. To find him, in your Address Book choose Find from the Tools menu, type **dav**, and press Enter. Outlook displays all names containing "dav", such as "Dave", "Davey", "David", and so on.

Tip

If you want to redisplay your entire address book after a search, select an address book from the Address Book drop-down list and click Name Only. Notice that Outlook now lists search results as a selection in case you want to return to your latest search results.

E-Mail a Name in the Address Book

① In the Address Book dialog box, click a contact to whom you want to send an e-mail message.

② Choose New Message from the File menu.

③ Type a subject.

④ Type your message text in the message body area.

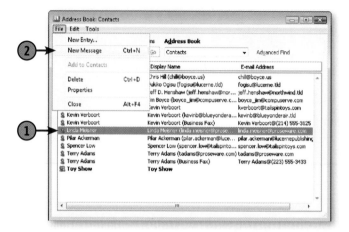

See Also

For more information on sending your message, see "Sending Messages" on page 69.

Tip

When you finish with the Address Book, close it by choosing Close from the File menu.

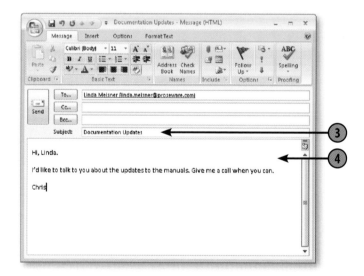

Working with Distribution Lists

A distribution list is a group of contacts that are related in some way. For example, you could create a distribution list that includes contacts working on the same project. Then when you need to send messages to the entire project team, simply select the distribution list for that project; Outlook sends the message to all the contacts in the list. Distribution lists are stored in the Contacts folder by default.

Create a Distribution List

1. In Outlook, choose New from the File menu.

2. Choose Distribution List from the New submenu.

3. Click in the Name field and type a name for the new distribution list.

4. Click Select Members in the ribbon to open the Select Members dialog box.

(continued on the next page)

Tip

You can share a distribution list with other users. To do so, open a new message and choose Item from the Insert menu. In the Look In list, select the folder, such as Contacts, that includes your distribution list.

In the Items list, select the distribution list you want to send. Click OK to attach the list to your new message.

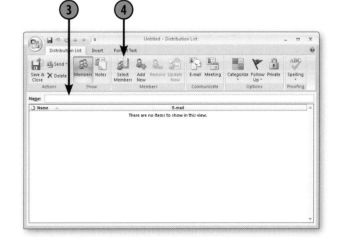

Create a Distribution List (continued)

⑤ From the Address Book drop-down list, select the address book that contains the names you want to add to the distribution list.

⑥ Click in the Search text box and type a name you want to add to the distribution list, or choose a name from the list that appears in the Name field.

⑦ Click Members to copy the name to the address list text box.

⑧ Click OK when your list is complete.

⑨ Click Save & Close.

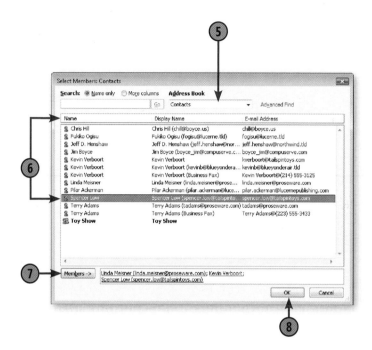

Tip

You can add existing contacts to a distribution list, and also add other addresses for recipients who are not in your existing contacts.

Use a Distribution List

1 In Outlook, click New from the Standard toolbar to start a new e-mail message.

2 Click To.

3 From the Name list, click the distribution list you want to use to address your e-mail message.

4 Click To.

5 Click OK.

Caution

When you use a distribution list, everyone on the list receives the same message. If you want to send a message to only a select few on the list, such as a confidential message that only specific recipients should read, create a new distribution list for these recipients, or select the recipients individually in the Select Names dialog box.

See Also

To learn how to send your message, see "Sending Messages" on page 69.

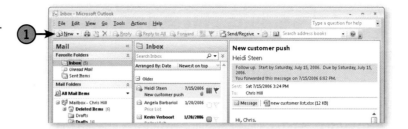

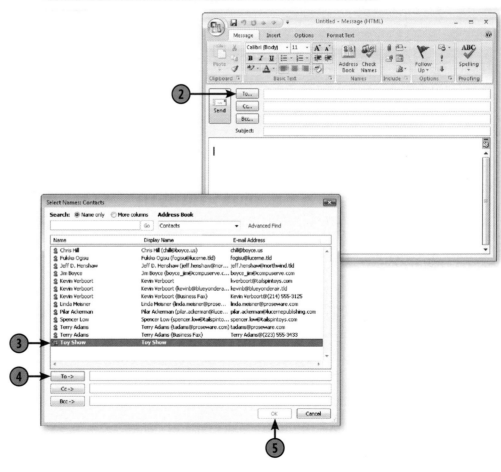

Changing Message Text

After you create a message and before you send it, you should proofread it for errors or omissions. If you discover a typographical or other error, you can edit it the same as you would a word-processing document. You can use familiar commands like Copy and Paste or operations like drag and drop to edit your text.

Edit Your Message

1. In Outlook, create a new mail message with recipients, a subject, and message text.

2. To change the recipient, click To.

3. In the Select Names dialog box, click a name in the Name list and click To to add it to the Message Recipients list.

(continued on the next page)

See Also

If you need to modify a contact's information, such as the e-mail address or name, you can do so in the Contacts folder. See "Updating an Existing Contact" on page 118.

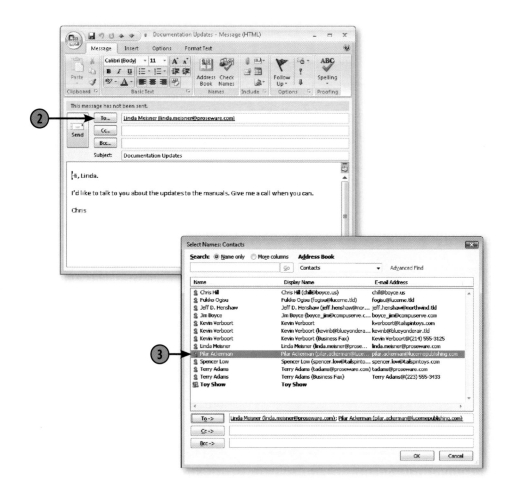

Edit Your Message *(continued)*

④ Click a name in the Message Recipients list and press Delete or Backspace to remove that person from the list.

⑤ Continue adding or deleting recipients until your recipient list includes all those you want to send the message to.

⑥ Click OK.

⑦ Click in the Subject line where you want to change text.

⑧ Click in the message body area where you want to change text.

⑨ Add or delete text as needed.

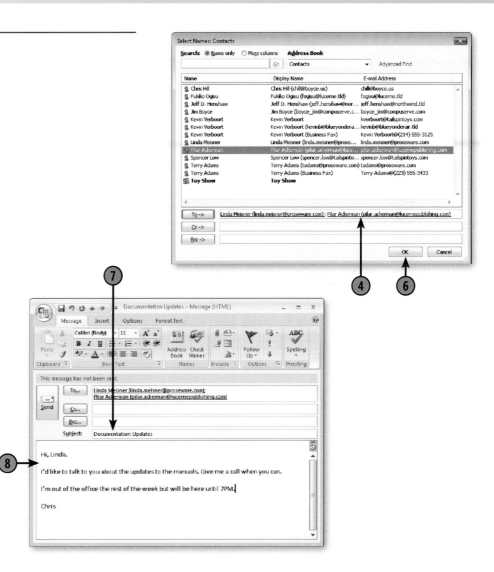

Move and Copy Message Text

(1) Display the message containing the text you want to move or copy.

(2) Select the text you want to move or copy.

(3) Drag the text to a new location. Or, to copy the text, hold down Ctrl as you drag the text.

(4) Drop the text.

Tip

Message text can be moved or copied within a message, between different messages, and between Outlook and other applications. For example, if you have a selection of text you want to use in several messages, you can select the text and press Ctrl+C to copy the text to the Clipboard, click in the body of each new message, and press Ctrl+V to paste the text into each message. You can also use the Copy and Paste buttons on the Message tab of the ribbon to copy and paste text.

Try This!

You can drag text from one message to another. Open both messages and position them so you can see both windows. Select the text you want to move and drag it to the other message window. Release the mouse button.

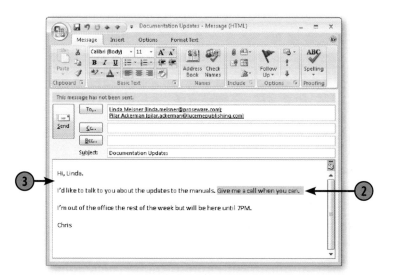

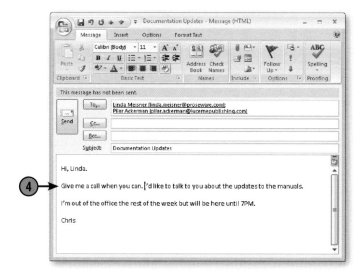

Formatting Message Text

Outlook lets you format text so that it looks more attractive to you and your recipients. For example, you can apply bold, italic, underline, colors, and other rich formatting to your mes-sages. You also can add HTML formatting to your messages, including tables, hyperlinks, heading levels, and more.

Use a Rich Text or HTML Message Format

① Create a new message, and add some text.

② Click the Options tab in the ribbon.

③ Choose HTML or Rich Text from the Format group on the ribbon.

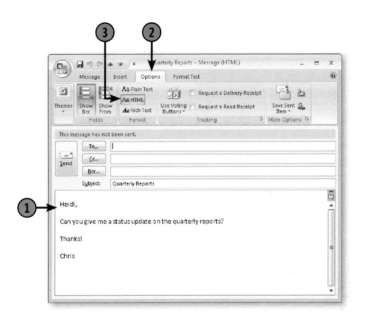

Tip ✓

Outlook 2007 uses Microsoft Office Word as the e-mail editor. There is no built-in Outlook editor as in previous versions of Outlook.

Caution !

If you add a hyperlink to a message, your recipient will need access to that site or document. For example, if the document you specify in the hyperlink is on the Internet, your recipient must have Internet access. Likewise, if your link is to a document you have stored locally on your hard drive, your recipient must have share privileges to that document.

Caution !

Some recipients may not be able to handle rich-formatted text. In these cases, the formatted text you see in your message window will appear to your recipients as plain text or be converted to unrecognizable characters.

Tip ✓

To add a hyperlink to an e-mail message, type the hyperlink in your message and Outlook converts it to a live link that your recipient can click. For example, you can add a hyperlink to the Microsoft Web site by typing *www.microsoft.com*.

Add Formatting to a Message

1. Select the text you want to format.

2. Click the Format Text tab on the ribbon.

3. Click Bold in the Font group to bold the text.

4. Click Italic to italicize the text.

5. Click Underline to underline the text.

6. Select a font name from the Font drop-down list to change the text font.

(continued on the next page)

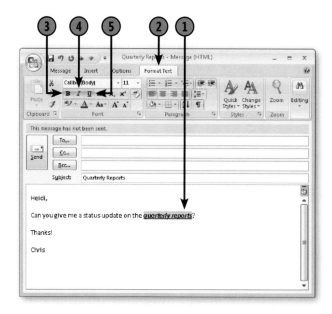

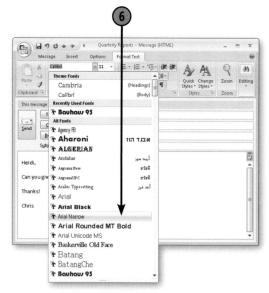

Add Formatting to
a Message *(continued)*

7 Select a color from the Font Color
drop-down list to change the text
font color.

8 Select a value from the Font Size
drop-down list to change the text
font size.

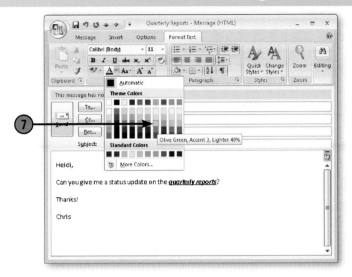

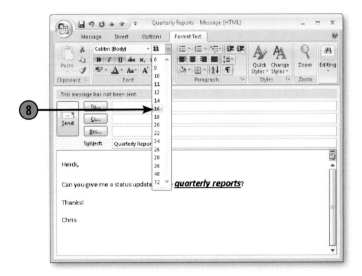

Using Signatures

A signature is boilerplate text or a file that is attached to any new messages you compose. The signature appears at the bottom of your messages, much like the signature that you would write on paper documents. Often, the signature includes your phone number and other information.

Create a Signature

1 In Outlook, choose Options from the Tools menu.

2 In the Options dialog box, click the Mail Format tab.

3 Click Signatures to open the Signatures and Stationery dialog box.

(continued on the next page)

Tip

A common signature includes your name, title, company name, address, phone number, and e-mail address.

Tip

You can create custom signatures for the type of e-mail message you create. For example, you can create a friendly signature for messages intended for family or friends.

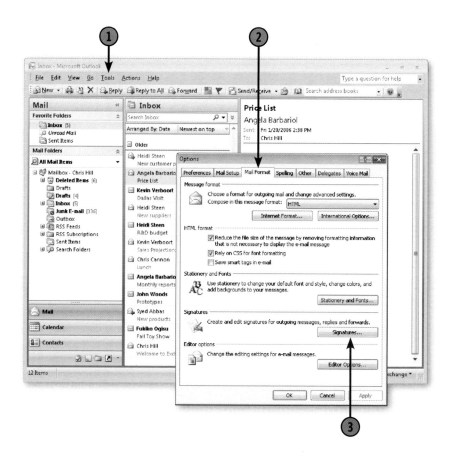

Create a Signature *(continued)*

④ Click New to open the New Signature dialog box.

⑤ Type a name for the signature and click OK.

⑥ Choose a font and font size.

⑦ Select font format options.

⑧ In the Edit Signature field, type the text you want to appear in your signature.

⑨ Add pictures or links to the signature, if desired.

⑩ Click OK twice to save your signature.

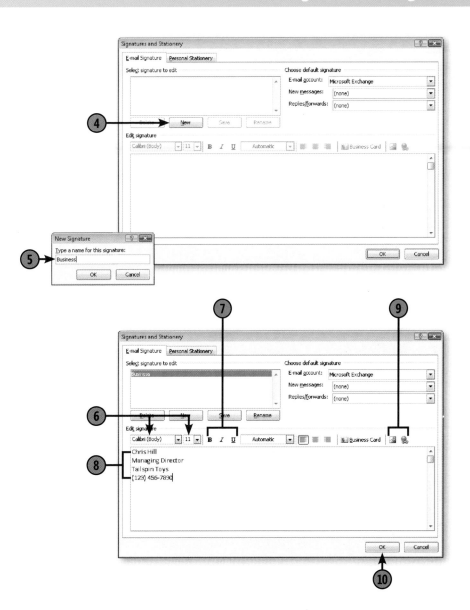

Tell Outlook to Use Your Signature

1. In Outlook, choose Options from the Tools menu.

2. Click the Mail Format tab.

3. Click Signatures to open the Signatures And Stationery dialog box.

4. From the E-mail Account drop-down list, select the account for which you want to assign the signature.

5. Select a signature from the New Messages drop-down list.

6. Click OK twice and close the Options dialog box.

Tip

If you want your signature to appear in messages you reply to or forward, select the appropriate signature from the Replies/Forwards drop-down list.

See Also

For information on replying to and forwarding messages, see "Replying to and Forwarding E-Mail" on page 83.

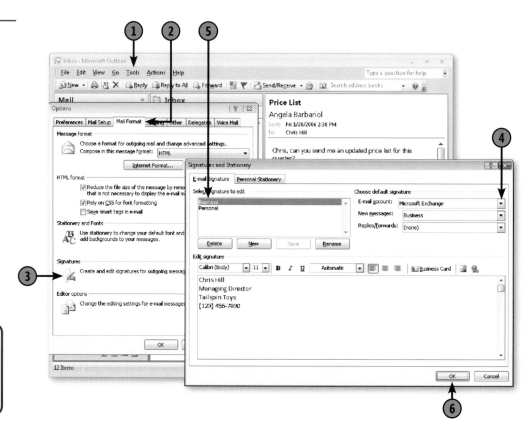

Working with HTML Stationery

Outlook includes a set of predefined designs and color schemes you can add to your rich text-formatted messages. These are known as HTML stationery. You can use or modify the stationery Outlook provides as-is. When you create a message, you can specify which stationery is used or set Outlook to use a default stationery pattern each time you create a new message. You can also specify the background image or color for an individual message.

Select Stationery

1. In Outlook, open the Inbox and choose New Mail Message Using from the Actions menu.

2. Choose More Stationery from the submenu.

3. Choose the stationery you want for your new message from the Theme Or Stationery dialog box.

4. Click OK.

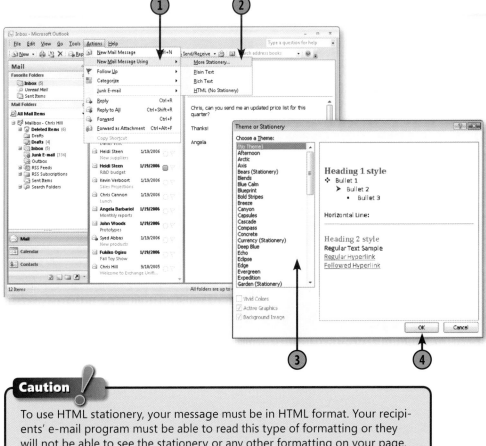

Tip

You can also use Word themes for messages. To do so, click the Themes button on the Options tab in the message form's ribbon. You can then select an existing theme from the gallery, browse for themes, save the current them, or search the Microsoft Office Online Web site for more themes.

Caution

To use HTML stationery, your message must be in HTML format. Your recipients' e-mail program must be able to read this type of formatting or they will not be able to see the stationery or any other formatting on your page.

Edit Stationery

① Choose Options from the Tools menu.

② Click the Mail Format tab.

③ Click Stationery And Fonts to open the Signatures and Stationery dialog box.

④ Click Theme and choose the stationery you want to edit, and then click OK.

⑤ From the Font drop-down list, choose Always Use My Fonts.

⑥ Choose the font options you want to modify.

⑦ Click OK.

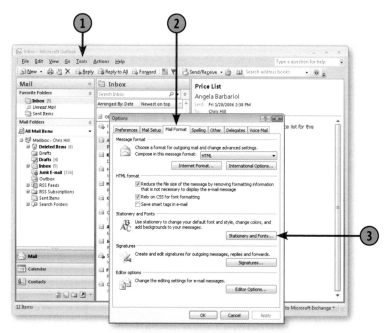

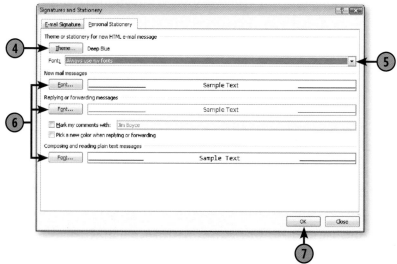

See Also

To learn how to change to HTML formatting, see "Use a Rich Text or HTML Message Format" on page 59.

Try This!

Some stationery uses only a picture or color. If you'd like to try editing one that uses both elements, edit the Citrus Punch stationery so it has a different background color.

E-Mailing a File

Sometimes when you create an e-mail message, you want to send along a file as well. Files sent with e-mail are called message attachments. When you send the message, the file goes along with the message so the recipient can open it on his or her computer. Outlook also allows you to insert a picture into your e-mail messages.

Insert a Picture

① To insert a picture in a message, you must choose either HTML or Rich Text format for the message. Open the message into which you want to insert a picture, and then choose HTML or Rich Text from the Format group of the Options tab on the ribbon.

② Click in the body of the message and then click the Insert tab on the ribbon.

③ Click Picture to open the Insert Picture dialog box.

④ Choose the picture you want to insert.

⑤ Click Insert.

⑥ The picture is now part of the message.

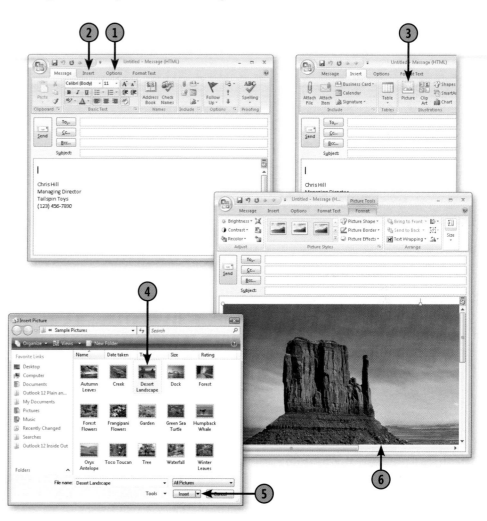

Attach a File

① Open a new message, and click the Insert tab on the ribbon.

② Click Attach File on the Attach group.

③ Click the file you want to attach.

④ Click Insert.

Caution

The recipient of an attached file must have an application on his or her computer that can open the attached file. If not, you may need to save the file in an agreed-on format before sending the file.

See Also

For information on saving and opening file attachments you receive from other people, see "Working with Attachments" on page 81.

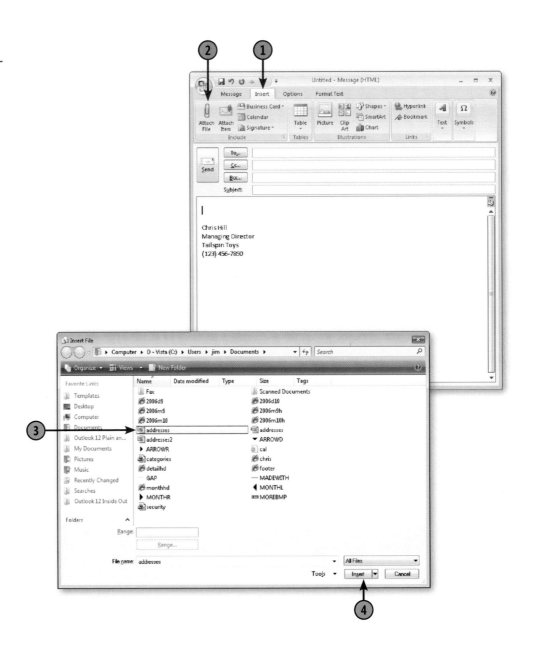

Sending Messages

When you send a message, it travels across the local area network or the Internet to the person you specify as the recipient. If you specify more than one recipient, Outlook sends a copy of the message to everyone you specify. By default, Outlook sends messages automatically as soon as they are placed in the Outbox. You also can configure Outlook to hold your messages in the Outbox until you're ready to send them. (Clicking Send places the message in the Outbox.)

Place a Message in the Outbox

1. Create a new message.
2. Click Send on the Message tab of the message form's ribbon.

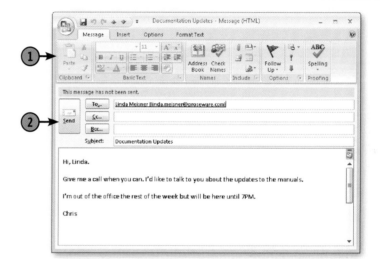

See Also

When you reply to or forward a message, you send it the same way you would send a new mail message. For more information, see "Replying to and Forwarding E-Mail" on page 83.

Caution

If Outlook is set up to send your messages as soon as you click the Send button, you will not have a chance to change anything in your message before it's routed to your recipients. Even if your message is incomplete or contains confidential information, you can't recall the message (unless you are using Exchange Server).

Transmit E-Mail
Messages Manually

(1) In Outlook, choose Options from the Tools menu.

(2) Click the Mail Setup tab.

(3) Clear the Send Immediately When Connected check box.

(4) Click OK and close the Options dialog box.

(5) Create a new message.

(6) Click Send to send the message to the Outbox folder.

(7) Click Outbox in the Navigation Pane.

(8) Confirm that a message is waiting in the Outbox folder.

(9) To send the message, click Send/ Receive on the standard toolbar.

See Also

For information on receiving e-mail messages, see "Receiving and Reading E-Mail" on page 73.

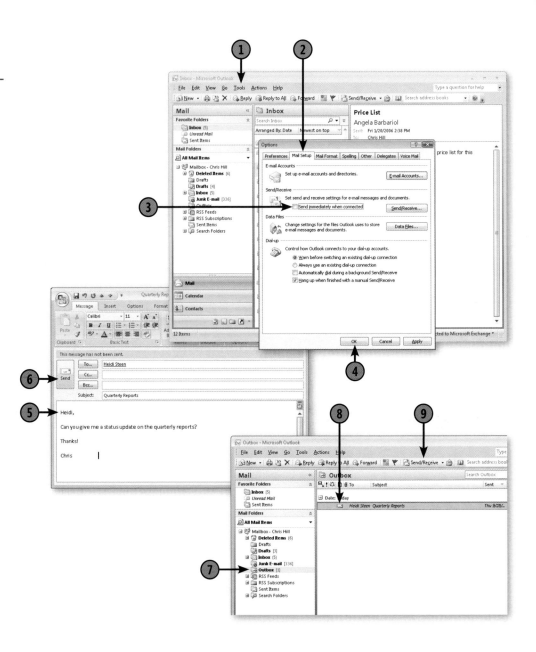

Reviewing Sent Messages and Drafts

When you send a message, Outlook stores a copy of it in the Sent Items folder. This folder enables you to keep track of all the messages you've sent to recipients. You can open this folder and review messages you've sent other users. Outlook also includes a Drafts folder that stores new messages you are working on but are not ready to send.

Open the Sent Items Folder

① Click the Mail button on the Navigation Pane.

② Click the Sent Items folder in the Navigation Pane.

③ Review the contents of the Sent Items folder.

Try This!

Create and send a few messages to others. Now open the Sent Items folder to see how the sent messages appear there.

Open the Drafts Folder

① Create a new message and add a recipient, subject line, and message text.

② Click the Office button

③ Choose Save.

④ Click Close from the Office menu.

⑤ Click the Drafts folder in the Navigation Pane. Your saved message is displayed.

See Also

You can move a message or group of messages from the Drafts folder to the Outbox folder without opening them first. To learn how to move items to different folders, see "Organizing with Folders" on page 211.

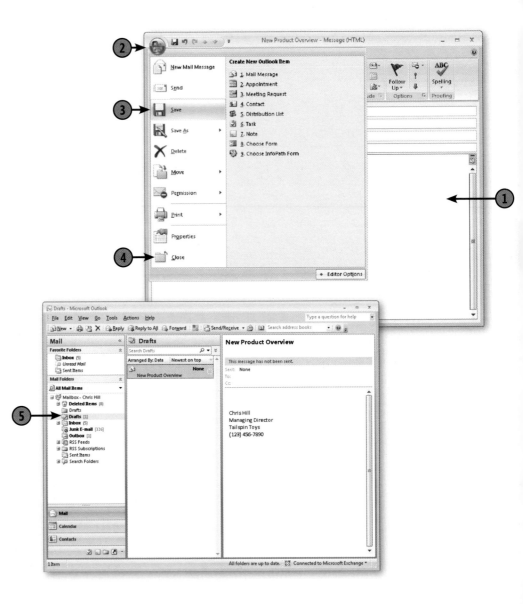

5

Receiving and Reading E-Mail

To receive e-mail messages that have been sent to you, Microsoft Office Outlook 2007 connects to an e-mail server on which messages are stored (such as servers located on a local area network or the Internet) and downloads the messages to your Inbox folder. From there you can read a message, reply, forward it to someone, flag it for later action, and open file attachments. In most cases, messages that you download are deleted from the server automatically after they are downloaded.

Outlook can also filter out junk e-mail by blocking mail that contains certain words or phrases or that arrives from certain addresses. You can adjust these filters to block mail from unwanted senders and let through the mail that you want to read. You also can set up Outlook Rules, which help you manage your messages by moving them to designated folders, flagging them, or otherwise processing messages in accordance with rules that you define.

This section shows you how to receive, read, reply to, follow up, and forward messages in Outlook. You learn how to manage your Inbox by deleting, saving, and printing messages. Finally, you learn how to handle junk mail, set up rules that personalize your e-mail experience, and work with e-mail attachments.

Receiving E-Mail

Outlook makes it easy for you to receive your incoming messages. You can schedule Outlook to download your new messages, or you can manually download new messages when you want.

Retrieve E-Mail Automatically

① Choose Options from the Tools menu.

② Click the Mail Setup tab.

③ Click Send/Receive.

④ Select the Schedule An Automatic Send/Receive Every *X* Minutes option.

⑤ Type the number of minutes between each download.

⑥ Click Close, and then close the Options dialog box.

⑦ Messages that appear in boldface are ones that you have not read yet.

⑧ The next time you start Outlook, it downloads any new messages. You can view them by clicking the Inbox folder.

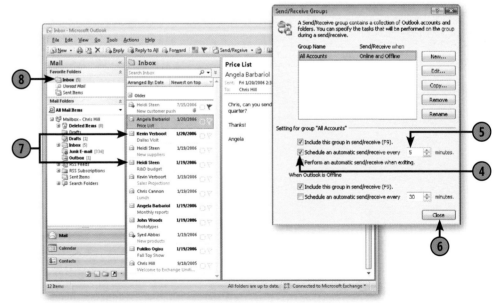

Retrieve E-Mail Manually

① Click Send/Receive on the Standard toolbar.

② Click the Inbox icon on Navigation Pane to see your new messages.

Tip

If you have Outlook configured for several e-mail message services, such as a Microsoft Exchange server and an Internet e-mail service, or two different Internet mail servers, clicking Send/Receive in the Standard toolbar downloads new messages from all these services. If you want to download messages from only one service, click the down arrow beside the Send/Receive button on the toolbar and then select a service from the Send and Receive submenu.

Tip

The total number of e-mail messages in your Inbox folder appears on the status bar, and the number of unread messages appears next to the Inbox icon in the Navigation Pane.

Reading E-Mail

After you receive a message in your Inbox folder, you can preview it or read its contents. The Inbox folder displays the sender's name, the message subject, the date the message was received, the size of the message, and whether the message has an attachment.

Locate New Messages

① Click the Mail button on the Navigation Pane to display your new messages.

② Choose Reading Pane from the View menu, then choose Bottom from the submenu.

③ Click the Received column to sort your new messages by the date you received them. Messages you have not read appear in boldface.

Try This!

Click the Received column once. If the most current date is at the top of the list, then you are sorting from the most current date received to the earliest date received. Click the Received column again to reverse the order of sorting, from the earliest date to the most current.

Tip

If the Reading Pane is displayed at the right, you can click Newest on Top or Oldest on Top to change the sort order for messages in the Inbox.

Tip

To find a message from a specific sender, click the From column. This sorts messages alphanumerically based on the sender's name.

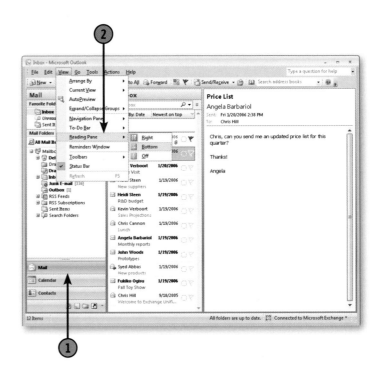

Open Message Items

1 Click the Inbox icon on the Navigation Pane to display your new messages.

2 Click the message you want to read to show its contents in the Reading Pane.

3 To open a message in its own window, double-click the message.

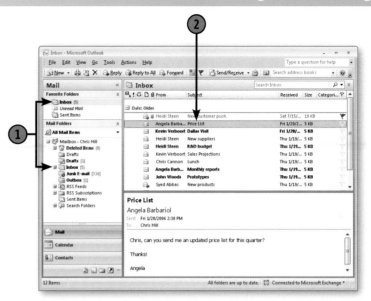

Tip

To turn the Reading Pane off, choose Reading Pane from the View menu, and choose Off from the submenu. To turn it back on, choose Right or Bottom from the Reading Pane menu.

Try This!

You can have Outlook display a few lines of each message by choosing AutoPreview from the View menu. This shows the first few lines of the messages in the Inbox folder.

Managing the Inbox Folder

Over time, your Inbox folder can quickly get jumbled with hundreds of messages. This makes finding messages more difficult and takes up hard drive space. You can reduce these problems by managing your Inbox folder. Some of the administrative tasks you can perform include deleting unneeded messages, saving important messages, and printing a copy of a message to read or store in hardcopy format.

Delete Unneeded Messages

 Click the Inbox icon on the Navigation Pane to display messages in your Inbox folder.

② Select the message you want to delete.

③ Click Delete on the Standard toolbar.

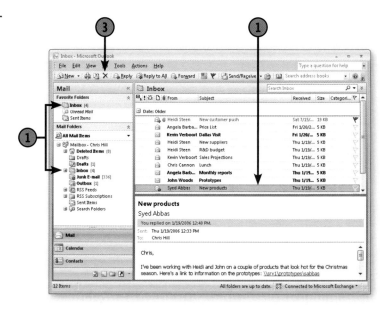

 Caution

Outlook does not ask if you are sure you want to delete a message. Make sure that you want to delete the message before you press Delete or choose the Delete command.

Tip

Deleted messages are moved to the Deleted Items folder and can be moved back to your Inbox folder if necessary. If you delete messages from the Deleted Items folder, those items are generally gone for good (unless you had copied them to another folder). If you are using Exchange Server, however, you can recover deleted items up to a period of time set by the mail administrator.

See Also

To learn more about managing items and folders, see "Managing Items and Folders" on page 201.

Save Important Messages

1. Click the Inbox icon on the Navigation Pane to display messages in your Inbox folder.

2. Select the message you want to save by clicking on it.

3. Choose Save As from the File menu.

4. If you want to save the message with a different name than the message subject, click in the File Name box and type a new name.

5. Click Browse Folders and choose a folder in which to store the message.

6. Click Save.

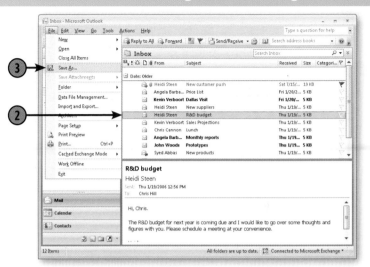

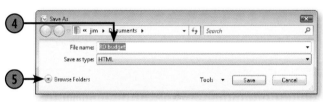

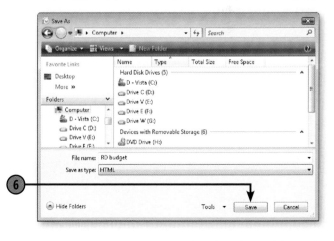

Tip

To save the message in a format other than message format (.msg), click the Save As Type drop-down list and choose the format type. You can save messages in text, HTML, Outlook template, and message format. This makes it handy when you want to open the message in another application, such as a word processor or Internet Web browser. Note that you can't save a plain text message in HTML.

Caution

When you save a message in a format other than .msg, the formatting of the message itself may change. If this is the case, you may find it difficult to read the message without modifying it.

Print a Copy of a Message

① Display or select a message in your Inbox folder.

② Choose Print from the File menu.

③ Click the Name drop-down list, and select the printer you want to use.

④ Click the Print Style option you want.

⑤ Click OK.

Tip

Clicking Print on the Standard toolbar sends the message to the default printer using the default settings.

Tip

If you want to see a preview of what your message will look like before printing it, choose Print Preview from the File menu.

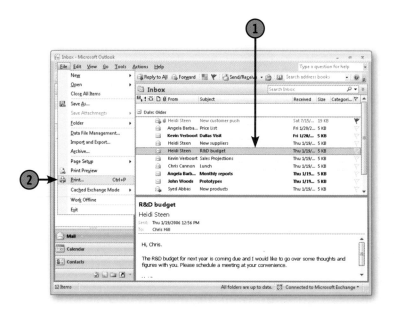

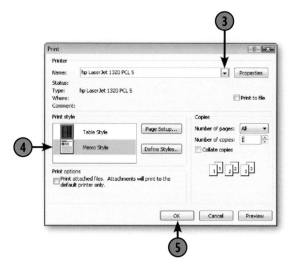

Working with Attachments

When you receive an e-mail attachment, you can open it directly from the message, save it to your hard drive and open it from there, or print it straight from the message to a printer. Messages that have attachments display a paper clip icon to the left of the message author's name or below the message received date, depending on the location of the Reading Pane and the width of the display.

Open an Attachment

① Click the Inbox icon on the Navigation Pane to display messages in your Inbox folder.

② Click the message with the attachment.

③ Double-click the attachment in the Attachments field.

④ If asked if you want to open or save the attachment, click Open.

Caution

Some files that you receive from another user, such as programs, Web pages, and script files, can be infected with a computer virus. You should save all executable files to your system and run an antivirus program that checks the file for a virus before you open it. If you receive an attachment from someone you do not know (as happens a lot with junk e-mail), you should never open it. Just delete the message.

See Also

For information on attaching files to messages you send, see "E-Mailing a File" on page 67.

Tip

To open an attachment, you must have an application that supports the attached file. For example, if you receive a PowerPoint file (.ppt or .pptx), you must have PowerPoint, the PowerPoint Viewer, or some similar application installed on your system to view the file.

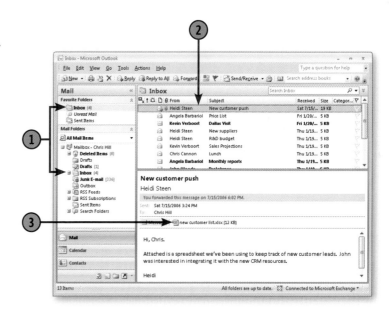

Save an Attachment

① Click the Inbox icon on the Navigation Pane to display messages in your Inbox folder.

② Click the message with the attachment.

③ Right-click the attachment in the Attachment field.

④ Choose Save As from the submenu.

⑤ Click Browse Folders.

⑥ Choose the folder where you want to save the file.

⑦ Make any necessary changes to the file name. The default file name is the one given by the sender when he or she initially attaches the file to the message.

⑧ Click Save.

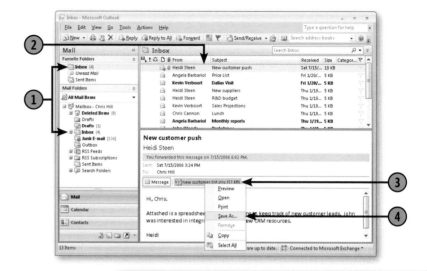

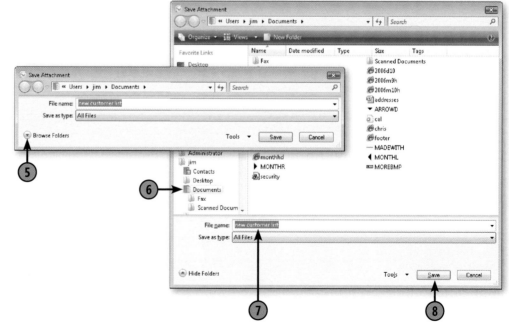

Replying to and Forwarding E-Mail

When you receive a message, you can reply directly back to the sender. You also have the option of forwarding the message or sending a response to everyone who receives the message. When you reply to a message, Outlook keeps the original message text and lets you add your new text above the original text. The sender's name becomes the recipient name, and the subject line begins with "RE:" to denote that the message is a reply.

Reply to an E-Mail Message

(1) Click the Inbox icon on the Navigation Pane to display messages in your Inbox folder.

(2) Click the message to which you want to reply.

(3) Click Reply on the Standard toolbar.

(4) Click in the space above the original message line, and type your reply.

(5) Click Send.

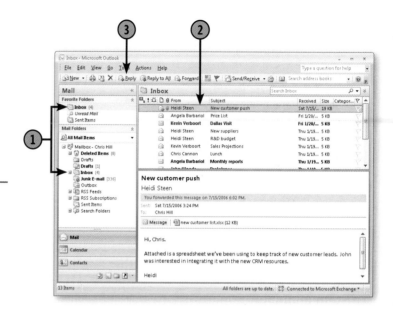

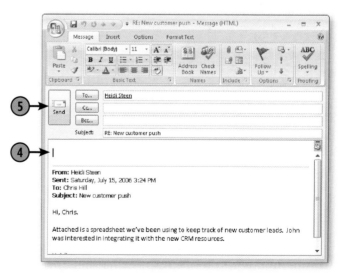

Tip

When you reply to messages that have attachments, the reply message does not include the attached file.

Tip

To reply to all recipients of a message, click Reply To All on the Standard toolbar.

Forward an E-Mail Message

① Click the Inbox icon on the Navigation Pane to display messages in your Inbox folder.

② Click the message you want to forward.

③ Click Forward on the Standard toolbar.

④ Add the address to which you want to forward this message.

⑤ Click in the space above the original message line, and type a message, if desired.

⑥ Click Send.

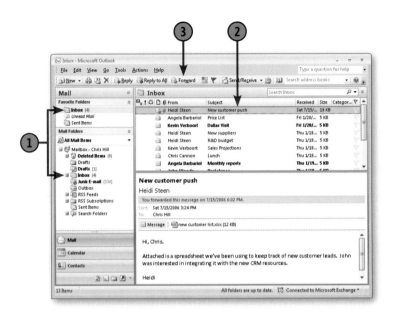

Tip

When you forward messages that have attachments, the forwarded message includes the attached file.

See Also

For information on addressing messages, see "Writing an E-Mail Message" on page 48.

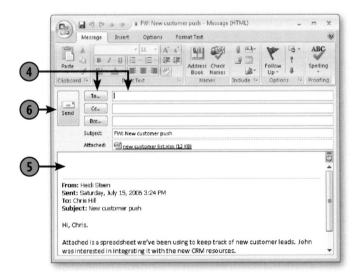

Handling Junk Mail

Just like the junk mail that you receive in your postal mailbox, you probably get too many junk e-mail messages (also known as *spam*) in your Outlook Inbox. Outlook makes it easy to set up mail filters that can sort your incoming mail so that junk mail is moved to its own folder, flagged, or deleted. Outlook also allows you to turn on mail filters so only specific messages are displayed in the Inbox.

Turn on Junk E-Mail Filters

1. Choose Options from the Tools menu.

2. Click Junk E-mail on the Preferences tab.

3. Choose a junk filtering level.

4. Choose other mail security options as desired.

5. Click OK twice.

See Also

For more information on setting rules and filters, see "Working with the Rules Wizard" on page 88.

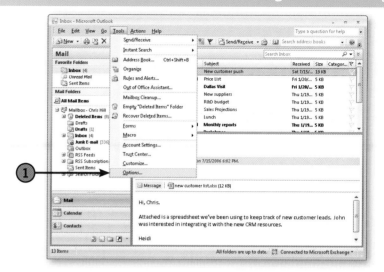

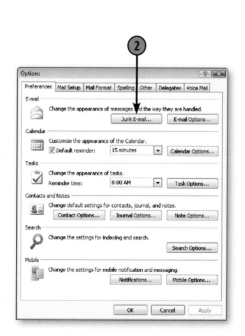

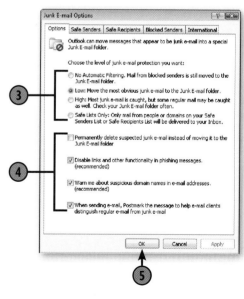

Add to the Junk Mail Senders List

① In the Inbox folder, click a message from a person who you want to add to the junk mail senders list.

② Select Junk E-mail on the Actions menu.

③ Choose Add Sender To Blocked Senders List from the submenu. A message box may appear telling you that the sender has been added to the junk e-mail list. Click OK.

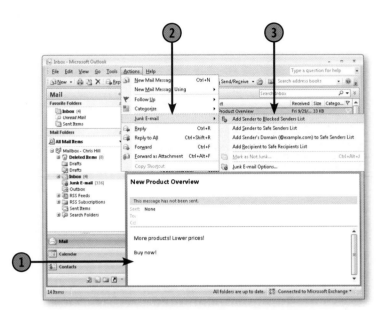

Fine-tune the Junk Mail Filter

① Choose Options from the Tools menu.

② Click Junk E-mail on the Preferences tab.

③ Click the Blocked Senders tab.

④ To remove a sender from the Junk Mail list, select a name and click Remove.

⑤ To add a sender to the Blocked Senders list, click Add.

⑥ Type the e-mail address or domain of the junk mail sender.

⑦ Click OK.

Tip

You can block an entire domain, if needed. Blocking a domain blocks all messages from all addresses in that domain.

See Also

For more information on setting rules, see "Working with the Rules Wizard" on page 88.

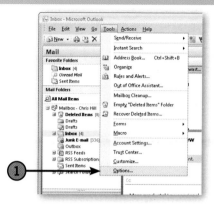

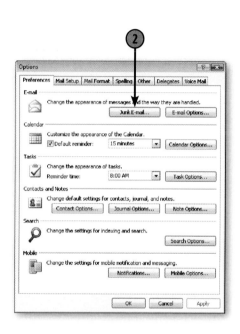

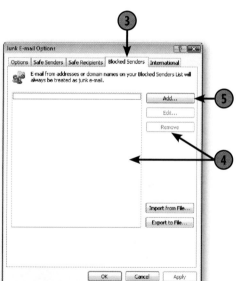

Working with the Rules Wizard

Outlook makes it easy to manage your e-mail by using rules. Rules are actions that Outlook performs on your messages to organize them. Once you have Outlook rules set, many management tasks are taken care of automatically when your new messages arrive. To make setting up rules painless, Outlook includes a Rules Wizard that walks you though the process of creating a rule by referring to a message you have already received. You can also create a rule from scratch.

Create a Rule Based on a Message

1 In the Inbox folder, right-click the message on which you want to base the new rule.

2 Click Create Rule on the shortcut menu to display the Create Rule dialog box.

(continued on the next page)

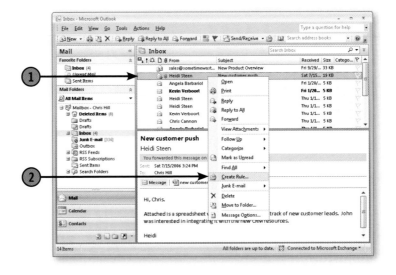

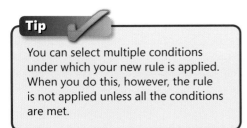

Tip

You can select multiple conditions under which your new rule is applied. When you do this, however, the rule is not applied unless all the conditions are met.

Create a Rule Based on
a Message *(continued)*

③ Choose the condition(s) to apply to the rule.

④ Choose the action you want Outlook to perform on messages that match the condition(s). For example, select the Move The Item To Folder option.

⑤ Click Select Folder.

⑥ Choose the folder to which you want the messages moved.

⑦ Click OK twice.

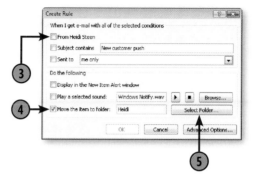

Tip

The conditions and actions available in the Create Rule dialog box are just some of the ones you can use in Outlook. The Rules Wizard, which you access by choosing Rules And Alerts from the Tools menu, offers many additional conditions and actions for message-processing rules.

Create a Rule from Scratch

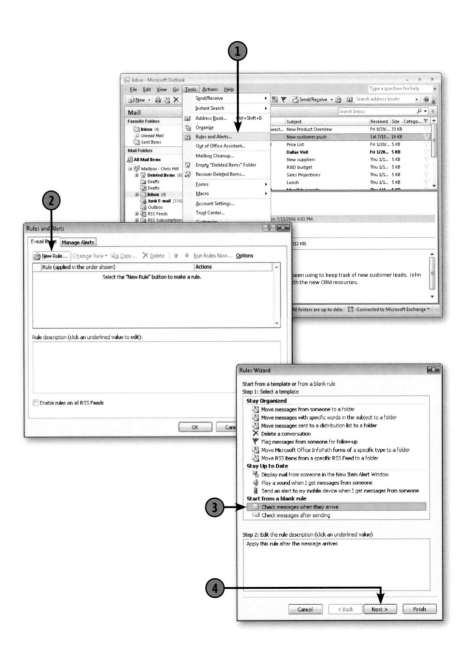

① With the Inbox folder displayed, choose Rules and Alerts from the Tools menu.

② Click New Rule.

③ Click Check Messages When They Arrive under Start From A Blank Rule.

④ Click Next.

(continued on the next page)

To run rules manually, click Run Now on the Rules Wizard dialog box. Select the rules you want to run, and click Run Now again.

Create a Rule from
Scratch *(continued)*

⑤ Select the condition(s) under which you want the rule applied, and then click Next.

⑥ If the condition requires additional configuration, click the link in the Step 2 field and enter the information.

⑦ Click Next.

⑧ Select what you want to do with the message.

⑨ If the action requires further configuration, click the link in the Step 2 field and enter the required information.

⑩ Click Next.

⑪ Select exceptions to the rule.

⑫ Click Next.

⑬ Type a name for your rule.

⑭ Select Turn On This Rule.

⑮ Click Finish.

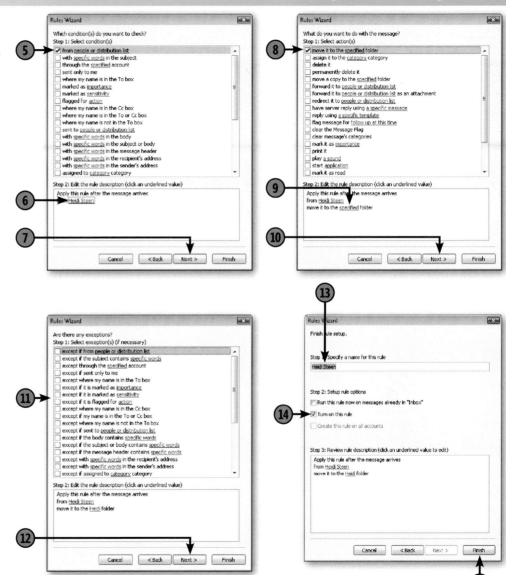

Following Up on a Message

When you receive a message, you may not have time or the information you need to reply to it. In such cases, you can flag a message to remind yourself to follow up on it later. You can designate different types of follow-up, including reminders to reply by e-mail, to forward the message to a third party, or to reply by telephone.

Flag a Message for Follow-Up

① In the Inbox pane, right-click the message you want to flag and choose Follow Up from the submenu.

② Select a type of follow-up, or click Add Reminder to set a reminder for a specific day and time (the remaining steps assume you click Add Reminder).

③ Select the follow-up action.

④ Place a checkmark in the Reminder check box.

⑤ Select a reminder date.

⑥ Set a time for the reminder, and then click OK.

Try This!

In the Flag For Follow Up dialog box, set a flag that is due today at 30 minutes from the current time. When the time expires, Outlook displays a message prompting you to follow up on the message.

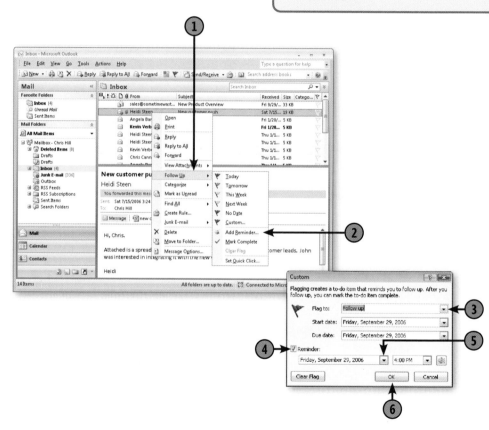

Tip

A small flag appears next to a message you flag.

Set Follow-Up Flag Status

1 In the Inbox pane, click the follow-up flag to clear or set the flag.

2 Right-click the message and choose Mark Complete.

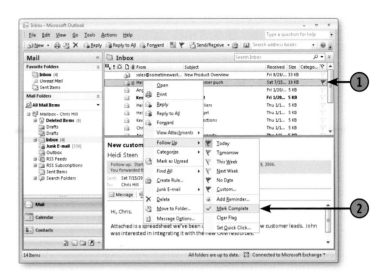

See Also

For information on replying to e-mail messages, see "Replying To and Forwarding E-Mail" on page 83.

Tip

When you clear a follow-up flag, a clear flag appears next to the message subject. If you later determine that you want to set the flag again, right-click the message, choose Follow Up from the submenu, deselect the Mark Complete option, and click OK.

6

Using RSS Feeds in Outlook

Rich Site Summary, now commonly called Really Simple Syndication (RSS), is an XML format that enables simplified publication of news feeds, listings, blogs, and other data. Microsoft Office Outlook 2007 adds RSS support directly in Outlook, enabling you to subscribe to and read RSS feeds from a variety of sources. For example, you might subscribe to your favorite news site, a sports site, and a blog or two. The data shows up in Outlook, organized neatly into folders. Reading an RSS item is as easy as reading an e-mail message.

Adding and using RSS feeds is very easy. It just takes a few clicks of the mouse to get your favorite information feeds to appear in Outlook. This section explains how to add and manage feeds, view feeds, and manage the folders that store the data in Outlook.

Adding an RSS Feed

Outlook makes it easy to add RSS feeds.
When your computer is connected to
the Internet, Outlook offers a page of
quick links you can use to add a feed
with a single click, or you can add feeds
by typing the URL for the feed.

Adding an RSS Feed from a Quick Link

1 Open Outlook and click RSS Feeds
in the Navigation Pane.

2 Click a link to add that feed
to Outlook.

Adding an RSS Feed Manually

1 Choose Account Settings from the
Tools menu.

(continued on the next page)

Adding an RSS
Feed Manually *(continued)*

② Click the RSS Feeds tab.

③ Click New.

④ Type the URL for the RSS feed and click Add.

⑤ Change the feed name if desired.

⑥ Select this option to Automatically Download The Full Item As An Attachment.

⑦ Click OK.

Tip

You don't need to type the URL for each RSS feed you add to Outlook. Instead, find the feed you want to add and highlight the link that points to the feed on the body of the Web page, or navigate to the feed and highlight the link in the browser's Address bar. Then press Ctrl+C to copy the link to the Clipboard. In the New RSS Feed dialog box, press Ctrl+V to paste the RSS link into Outlook.

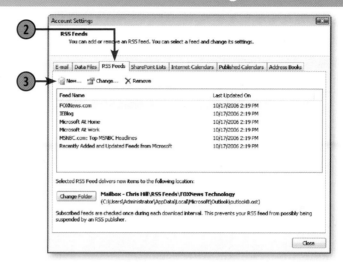

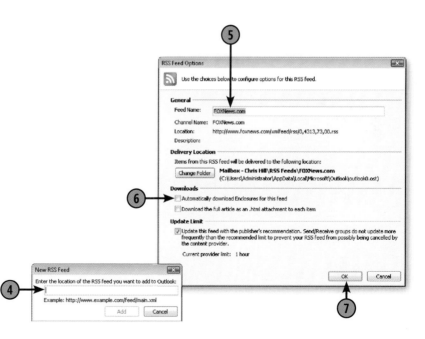

Viewing RSS Feeds

Because Outlook by default separates your RSS feeds into individual folders, you can easily locate and view content from a specific feed.

① In the Outlook Navigation Pane, click to expand the RSS Feeds folder.

② Click the feed you want to view.

③ Look through items to find the one you want to read and click it.

④ Preview the item in the Reading Pane.

⑤ Click to view the full item.

Tip

The Reading Pane displays a banner that, when clicked, lets you either display the full article associated with the item or download associated content.

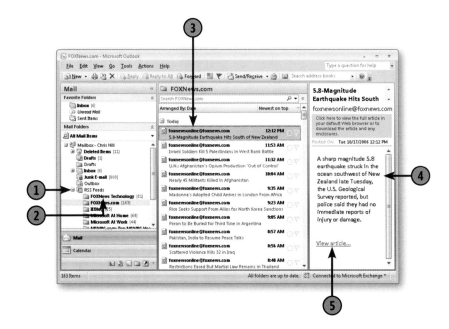

Managing Folders

When you add an RSS feed, Outlook creates a folder to contain the items downloaded from that feed. You can change the name or location of the folder when you add the feed. You can also change the folder name or location at any time after you add the feed. The capability to change folders lets you manage your RSS feeds in a folder structure that suits your needs.

Rename an RSS Folder

1 Click to expand the folder list under RSS Feeds in the Navigation Pane.

2 Right-click the folder and choose Rename.

3 Type a new name for the folder and press Enter.

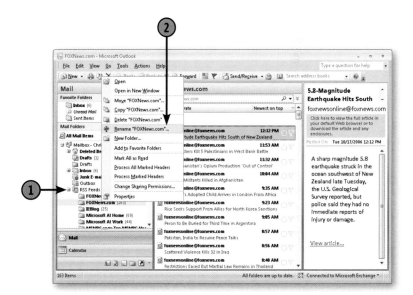

Tip

You can click on a folder name to select the folder, then click on it again and type a new name to rename the folder.

Use a Different Folder
(Change Folder Location)

(1) Choose Account Settings from the Tools menu.

(2) Click the RSS Feeds tab.

(3) Click Change Folder.

(4) Select an existing folder, or...

(5) Click New Folder to create a new folder for the feed.

(6) Click OK, then click Close.

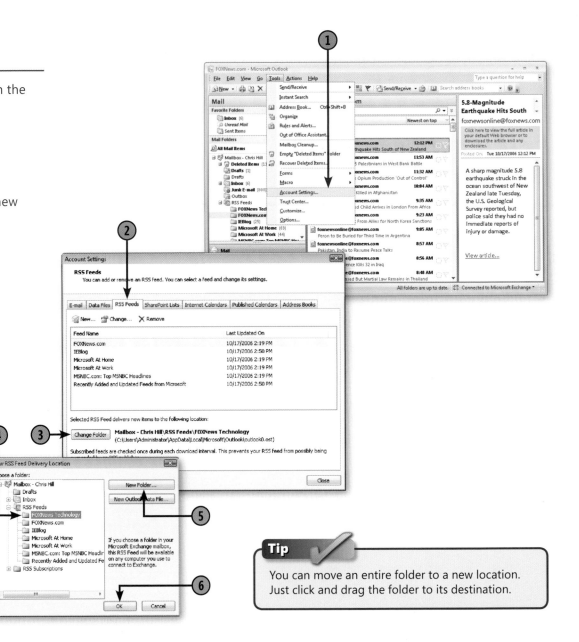

Tip

You can move an entire folder to a new location. Just click and drag the folder to its destination.

Managing Messages

RSS feed messages are much like e-mail messages you receive in your Inbox. You can mark them as read or unread, delete them, download full article content, move them between folders, and delete the items. You can also easily share a feed with others by sending the feed in an e-mail message. The recipient can then click an icon in the message to add the feed to his or her Outlook RSS subscriptions.

Mark and Unmark RSS Messages

(1) Right-click a message.

(2) Choose Mark As Unread to mark the message as unread. Choose Mark As Read to mark the message as having been read.

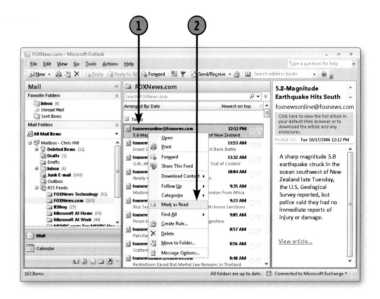

Move Messages
Between Folders

(1) Click the message you want to move.

(2) Drag and drop the message on the target folder, or...

(3) Right-click the item and choose Move To Folder.

(4) Select the target folder.

(5) Click OK.

Tip

You can copy a message rather than move it, preserving the message in the original location. To copy a message, right-drag the message to the destination and choose Copy from the pop-up menu.

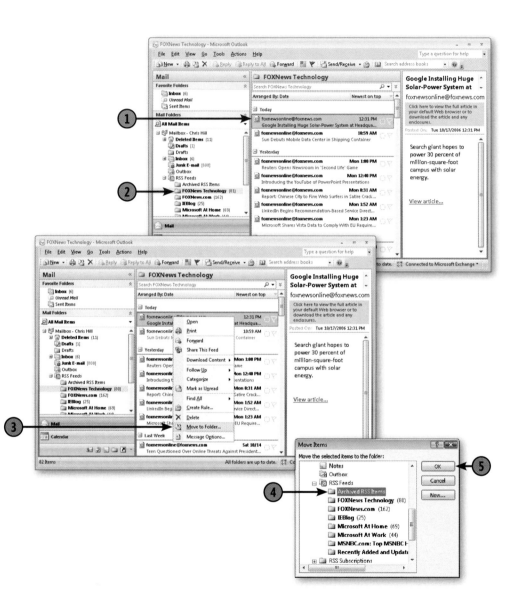

Download a Full Article

① Right-click a message and choose Download Article from the Download Content menu.

② After the article has downloaded, double-click the attachment to view the article in your Web browser.

Tip

Downloading an RSS article is useful when you want to keep a copy of the article on your computer. If you are only interested in reading the article but not keeping it, just click the View Article link in the Preview Pane to open the article in your Web browser. Or, open the RSS item and click the View Article link in the body of the item to view the article. Reading the article online rather than downloading it will save a little bit of disk space.

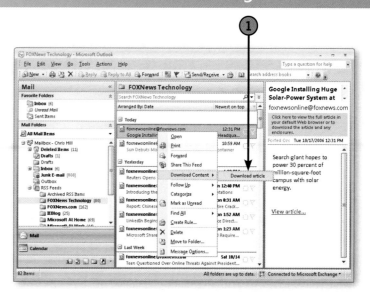

7

Working with Contacts

Staying in contact with others is part of life and an important task in business. Whether it's your best friend from high school, a client you've worked with for years, or a new customer, you need a way to store all the information about each one of them.

Microsoft Office Outlook 2007's Contact feature enables you to save personal and business contact information, including phone numbers, addresses, e-mail addresses, Web site information, and personal data. Instead of being a glorified card file to store your information in, the Contacts folder is a full-featured database that lets you use automatic dialing to call a contact, import data from other contact managers or databases (such as Microsoft Access), create new messages to a contact, set up distribution lists for contacts, and more. Outlook gives you several ways to view your contacts as well. For example, you can view contacts using address cards, group contacts by category, or list them by their phone numbers. As with other folders, Outlook also lets you create custom views.

This section explores the Contacts folder. In it you learn how to create and sort contacts and use them for a variety of tasks. You learn how to send e-mail messages to contacts, work with contacts in your address book, add files to a contact, and much more.

Adding a New Contact

You can add contacts to Outlook's Contacts folder in three ways: by typing new information about someone, by using information you've entered for another contact, or by using information from an e-mail message. In the latter case, for example, you can quickly create a new contact by using the information from a message that you've received.

Use E-Mail Message Information

① With the Inbox showing, select the message that has the contact information you want to save. If you don't have the Reading Pane displayed, open the message to access the From field.

② Right-click the name or address that appears in the From field.

③ Choose Add To Outlook Contacts from the shortcut menu that appears. A new contact card opens, with some of the new contact's information already entered.

(continued on the next page)

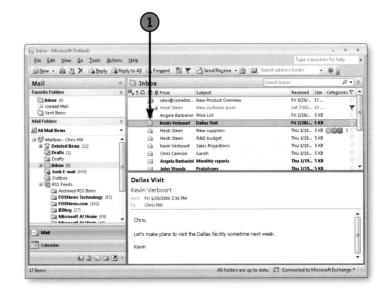

Tip

Depending on how the From field is filled out in an e-mail message, you may need to modify the Full Name field when you create a new contact from a mail message. For example, if the sender's name is not complete or does not appear at all, you need to manually enter the information in the address card.

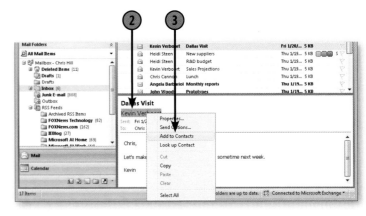

Use E-Mail Message Information *(continued)*

④ Type the pertinent information into the remaining fields.

⑤ Click Save & Close to save the contact information.

Try This!

Click Full Name on the address card to open the Check Full Name dialog box. In this box, fill in the complete name and any appropriate prefix (such as "Dr.") or suffix (such as "Jr."). Click OK.

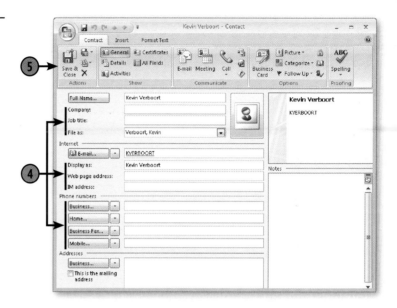

Use the Contact Window

1 Click the Contacts icon on the Navigation Pane to display the Contacts folder.

2 Double-click the contact you want to open.

(continued on the next page)

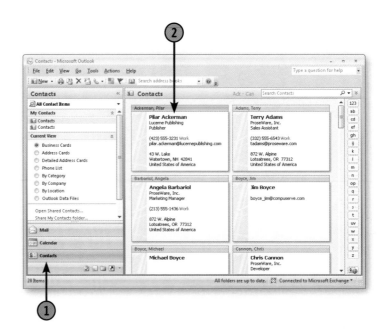

Caution

When typing a contact's e-mail address, be sure you type it correctly. An incorrect address will prevent your messages from being sent successfully. Take the time when typing a contact's e-mail address to double-check it for accuracy. You can, of course, change it later, but it's best to make sure it's correct now.

Tip

If you want to keep the Inbox open and also open Contacts, right-click Contacts on the Navigation Pane and choose Open in New Window.

Tip

To ensure the AutoDialer feature works correctly, type phone numbers as numbers, rather than using any acronyms or letters.

Use the Contact Window *(continued)*

③ Type information about your contact in the appropriate fields.

④ From the File As drop-down list, select one of the choices of how Outlook can display the contact's name, such as last name first, first name last, and so on.

⑤ Type any additional useful information in the Notes box at the bottom of the address card.

⑥ Click Save & Close to save your changes.

Tip

If the contact already exists in your Contacts folder, Outlook asks if you want to update the information in the existing contact with the new information.

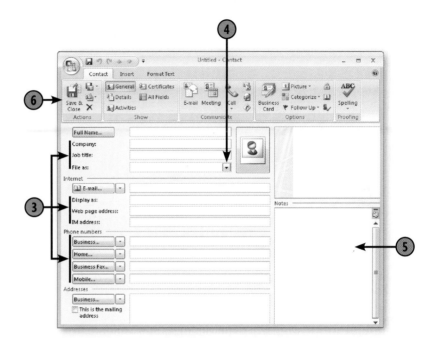

Inserting Items into a Contact Record

You can add Outlook items, application and document objects, and files to a contact by using the Item command on the Insert menu. For example, you can add an e-mail message to a contact for future reference, insert an attachment, or insert a Microsoft Excel worksheet. This enables you to access these items from the contact card. You can add a new, empty item and then modify it right in the Outlook item, or you can insert an existing document.

Add an Outlook Item

1. In an open contact, click in the Notes box.

2. Click the Insert tab on the ribbon.

3. Click Attach Item.

(continued on the next page)

See Also

For more information about Outlook items, see "Working with Outlook Items" on page 34.

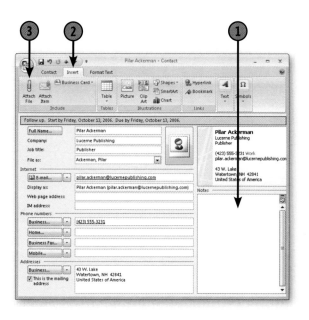

Add an Outlook Item *(continued)*

④ Click the Outlook folder in which the item you want to insert is located.

⑤ Select an item in the Items list.

⑥ Select the format of the item: Text Only, Attachment, or Shortcut.

⑦ Click OK to insert the item into the contact address card.

⑧ The item now appears with the contact.

⑨ Click the Contact tab on the ribbon, and click Save & Close.

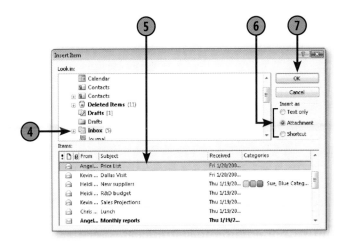

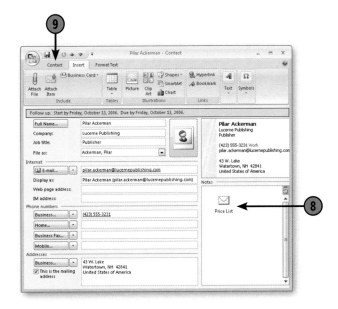

Add a File

1. Open a contact, and click the Insert tab on the ribbon.
2. Click the paperclip icon.
3. Select the folder in which the file you want to insert is located.
4. Select the file you want to insert.
5. Click Insert.
6. The file now appears with the contact.
7. Click the Contact tab on the ribbon, and click Save & Close.

Try This!

To remove a file from a contact, click the file and press Delete.

Tip

After you insert a file into a contact's card, you can open it to view, edit, or print it. To do this, double-click the file's icon in the address card to launch the file within its associated application.

Caution

As you add items, files, and objects to a contact, the size of that contact card increases. When you add several items, files, or objects to a contact, it takes longer for Outlook to open the card. You should limit the number of attachments you add to a contact.

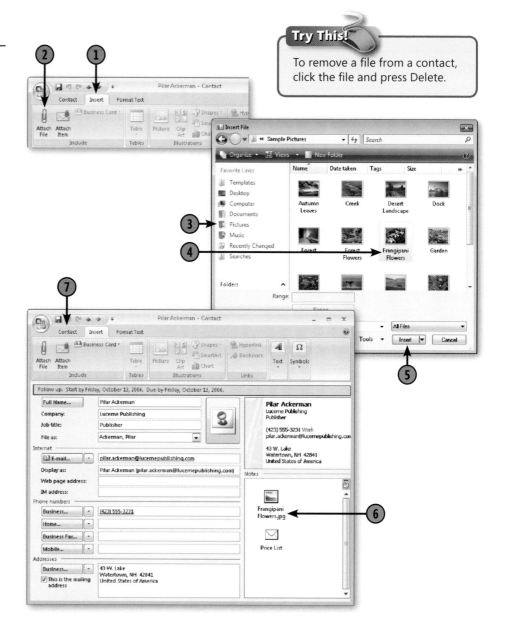

Viewing Your Contacts Folder

Outlook lets you view your contacts as a series of single address cards or all at once, moving through your Contacts folder as if it were an electronic phone book or address book. Another way to look at your contact information is through the Outlook Address Book, which lists contacts alphabetically.

Use the Contacts Folder

(1) Click the Contacts icon on the Navigation Pane.

(2) Choose Current View from the View menu. (You can also simply click a view in the Navigation Pane.)

(3) Select the view type you want to use to view the contact information in the Contacts folder. You can choose from the following list:

- Business Cards
- Address Cards
- Detailed Address Cards
- Phone List
- By Category
- By Company
- By Location
- By Follow-Up Flag
- Outlook Data Files

See Also

One task that no one wants to face is typing in all their contacts a second time. This is why it's a good idea to set up a backup schedule to make sure your contacts are backed up at least once a week. For information on backing up and restoring Outlook Contacts, see "Backing Up and Restoring a Data File" on page 226.

Try This!

To see how Outlook displays your contact information in different formats, select each of the views in the Current View drop-down list. When you see one that you like, such as the Detailed Address Cards, keep it so that the next time you open the Contacts folder that view is showing.

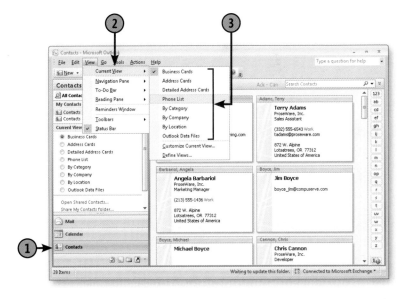

Add a Contact in the Address Book

① Choose Address Book from the Tools menu.

② Choose New Entry from the File menu.

③ Click New Contact in the New Entry dialog box.

④ Click OK.

⑤ Add the new contact information to the appropriate fields and click Save & Close.

See Also

For more information on using and modifying contact information via the Address Book, see "Working with the Address Book" on page 50.

Tip

You can add distribution lists to the Contacts folder using the Address Book. Rather than clicking New Contact in the Select The Entry Type dialog box, click New Distribution List. The new distribution list appears in the Contacts folder alongside individual entries.

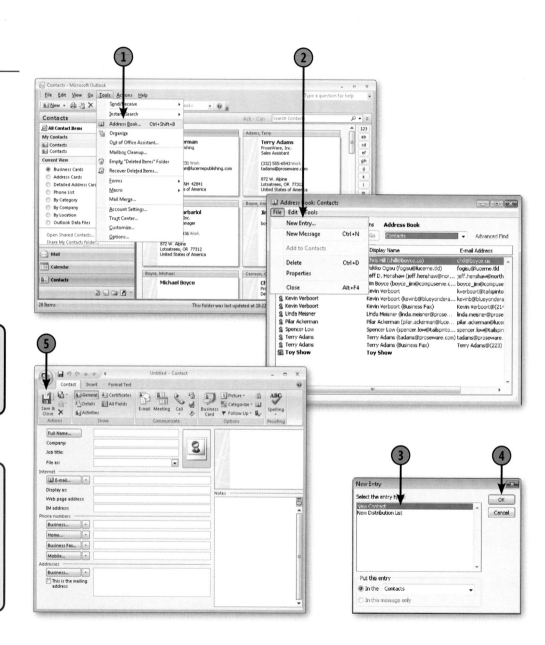

Viewing Contact Information

After you create a contact, you can view it in the Contacts folder or open it in its own address card. In the Contacts folder, you can see the contact's name, company, title, selected phone information, e-mail address, and postal address. To see a contact's full set of information, you must display the contact form. When you view the contact, you can print the information, view activities associated with a contact, and display a map to the address.

Print Contact Information

(1) Click the Contacts icon in the Navigation Pane.

(2) Double-click the contact you want to print.

(3) Click the Microsoft Office button, then choose Print from the Print menu.

(4) Verify options in the Print dialog box, and click OK.

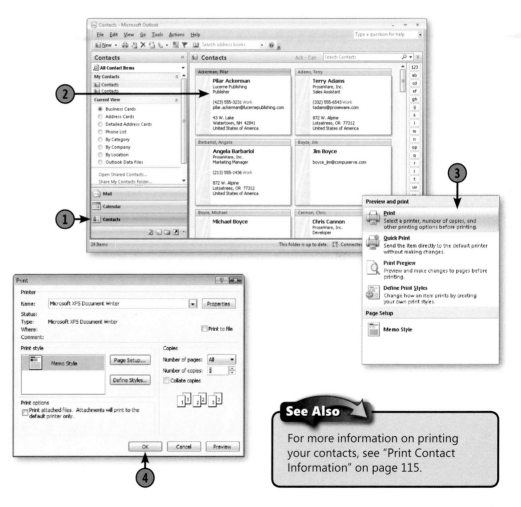

Tip

To print attachments inserted into the contact, first open the contact and choose Print from the File menu. Select Print Attached Files in the Print dialog box. The attachments open in their associated application (for example, an Excel worksheet opens in Excel) and print. The attachments print to the default printer, even if you select a different printer in the Outlook Print dialog box.

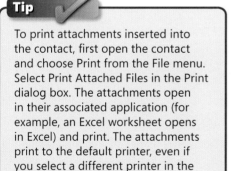

See Also

For more information on printing your contacts, see "Print Contact Information" on page 115.

Use the Activities Tab

① Click the Contacts icon on the Navigation Pane.

② Double-click the contact name you want to view.

③ In the ribbon, click Activities from the Show group.

④ Click the Show drop-down list.

⑤ Select the type of item you want to view.

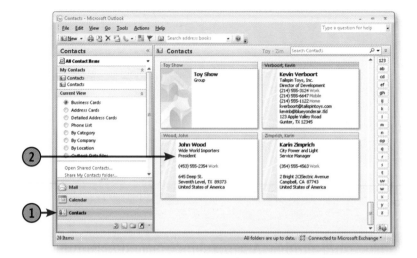

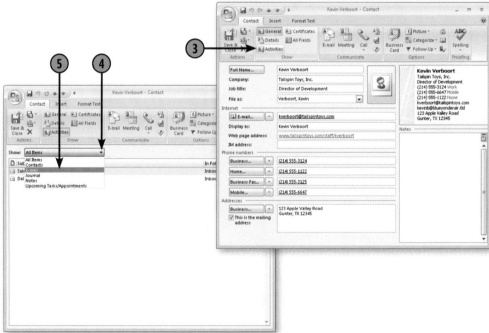

Tip

Searching for activities associated with a contact can take a long time if the contact has a long list of items associated with it. If it takes too long, you can stop the search at any time by clicking the Stop button on the right-hand side of the Activities tab.

Display a Map

1. Click the Contacts icon on the Navigation Pane.

2. Double-click the contact for which you want to display a map.

3. On the Contact tab of the ribbon, in the Communicate group, click Map.

4. View the map in your Web browser.

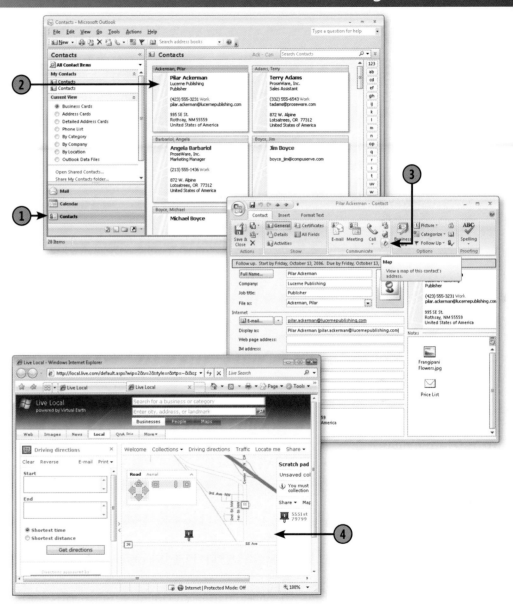

Tip

To see a map for an address, you must have Internet access.

Caution

Not all addresses are available from the Windows Live Local Web site. If the address you are looking for is not found, modify the information you enter on the search Web page. Click the Search button to begin the search again.

Updating an Existing Contact

You can store a great deal of information about a person or company in a single address card. For many contacts, however, you probably will start by typing only the most critical information. Later, you need to update the information. Outlook makes it easy to do. Simply open the Contacts folder, locate the contact you want to update, open the contact card for that person, and make your changes.

Use the Contacts Folder

1. Click the Contacts folder icon on the Navigation Pane.

2. Select Current View on the View menu, and then select a view type. Or simply click a view in the Navigation Pane to show that view.

3. Click in the scroll bar to navigate through the list of contacts.

4. Double-click a contact to open its form for viewing or modification.

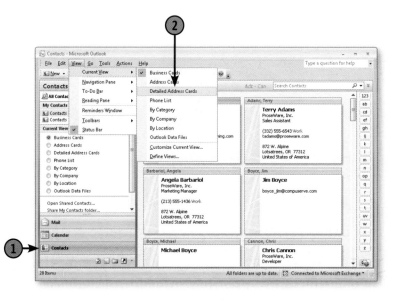

See Also

For information on using contacts in e-mail messages, see "Writing and Sending E-Mail" on page 47.

Tip

When viewing contacts using the Business Cards, Address Cards, and Detailed Address Cards views, you can click the letter buttons on the right side of the window to jump to contacts whose names start with that letter. For example, click the letter "m" to jump to contacts named "Mitchell," "Mosley," and so on.

Finding a Contact

Outlook makes it easy to find contacts. You can search for them using the Find tool, you can use the Find A Contact box, or simply scroll through the list of your contacts. With Outlook you don't even have to know the complete name of the person you are looking for, because searching for part of a name brings up any name that matches that string.

Scroll Through the Contacts Folder

① Click the Contacts folder icon on the Navigation Pane.

② Select Current View from the View menu, and then select Address Cards from the submenu, or click Address Cards in the Navigation Pane.

③ Move the scroll bar at the bottom of the Contacts folder to scroll through your contacts.

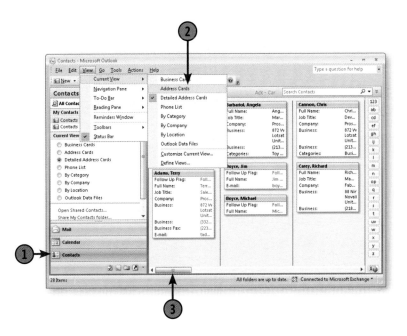

Caution

Be careful when viewing contacts in the Contacts folder. If you press Delete after clicking on a contact, you'll delete the contact. If this happens, select Undo Delete from the Edit menu.

Tip

If your Contacts folder is really large, scrolling through the list of contacts is not the most efficient way to locate a contact. Instead, use the Find A Contact box or the Find tool to locate the contact.

Use the Find A Contact Box

(1) Click the Contacts folder icon on the Navigation Pane.

(2) In the Find box, type part of the name of the contact you want to find.

(3) Press Enter.

(4) Select a contact.

(5) Click OK.

See Also

For information on finding names in the Address Book, see "Find a Name In the Address Book" on page 51.

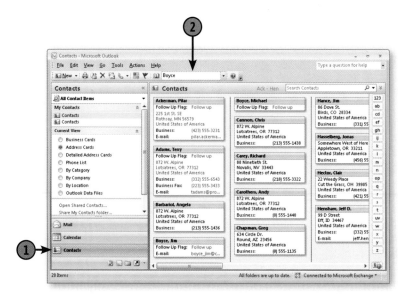

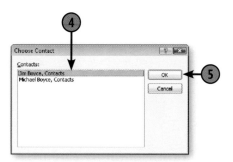

Use the Advanced Find Dialog Box

 Click the Contacts folder icon on the Navigation Pane.

 Choose Instant Search from the Tools menu, then select Advanced Find from the submenu.

③ Type a word or phrase in the Search For The Word(s) field.

④ Select the fields in which to search.

⑤ Click Find Now to search for contacts matching the search criteria.

Tip

Click New Search to clear your search results so you can begin a new one. You need to click OK when prompted that you'll lose the results of the previous search.

Tip

You can use the Advanced Find dialog box to find contacts using a number of search criteria. For example, you can search for contacts who have a specific e-mail address or domain name in the e-mail address. This is handy if you know that a contact has a domain name of @tailspintoys.com but are not sure of her name or e-mail address. Simply type **@tailspintoys.com** in the E-mail field, and press Enter.

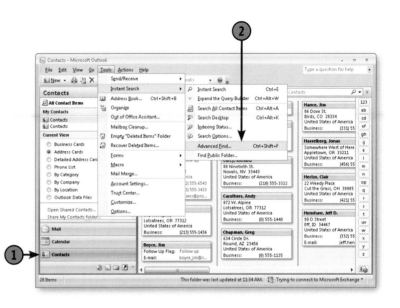

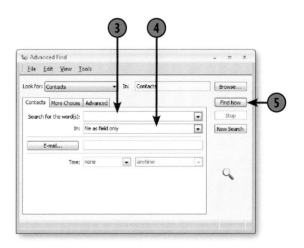

Organizing Your Contacts

When you have only a dozen or so contacts, finding and managing them is fairly easy. You can simply open the Contacts folder, scroll through the list and find what you're looking for. However, once the Contacts folder grows, you need to organize your contacts to make them easier to find and update. Outlook provides three ways to organize your contacts. You can use folders to store related contacts, use categories to set up relationships between contacts, or use views to sort contacts in ways that make sense to you.

Try This!

Once you create a folder for contacts, you can drag existing contacts to your new folder to organize them as necessary. For example, create a folder named "Project Team" in the Contacts folder. Open the Folder List in the Navigation Pane so you can see the new folder, but keep the focus on the Contacts folder. Drag members from your project team into the Project Team folder. You now can quickly see who is on your team by clicking this folder.

Use Folders

1. Click the Contacts icon on the Navigation Pane.

2. Choose Folder from the File menu, and then select New Folder from the submenu.

3. Type a name for the folder in the Name field.

4. Click the Folder Contains drop-down list, and select Contact Items.

5. Click OK.

(continued on the next page)

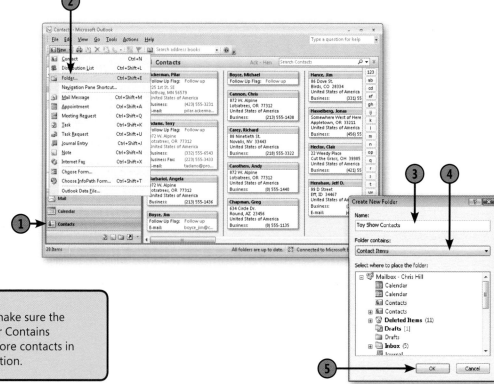

Caution

When you create a new folder for contacts, make sure the Contact Items option is selected in the Folder Contains drop-down list. If it is not, Outlook will not store contacts in the correct format and you may lose information.

Use Folders *(continued)*

6 Click Folder List on the Navigation Pane.

7 Click to expand the folder list to view the new folder.

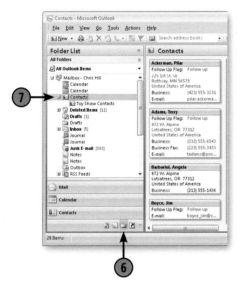

Use Categories

1 Click the Contacts icon on the Navigation Pane.

2 Right-click a contact, and select Categorize from the shortcut menu.

3 Select the category to which you want the contact to belong.

See Also

For more information on Outlook Categories, see "Using Categories" on page 202.

Tip

You can add your own categories and modify existing ones. Choose Categorize from the Actions menu, then choose All Categories to open the Color Categories dialog box, where you can add and modify categories.

Customize Views

1. Click the Contacts icon on the Navigation Pane.

2. Choose Current View from the View menu, then choose Customize Current View.

3. Click Fields to open the Show Fields dialog box.

4. Click a field in the Available Fields list.

(continued on the next page)

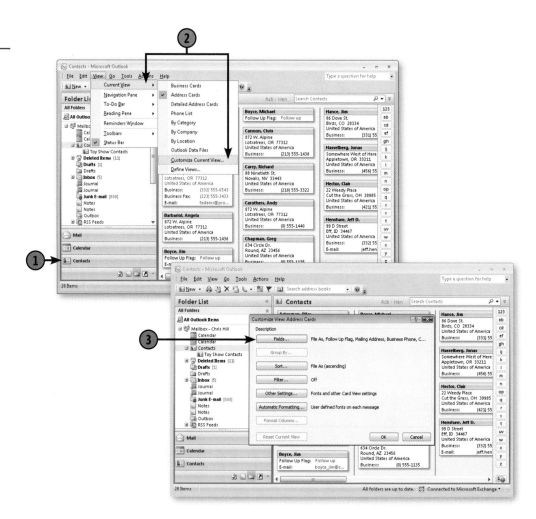

Tip

You can create and use customized views in any Outlook folder, not just the Contacts folder.

See Also

For more information on sorting contacts, see "Organizing Your Contacts" on page 122.

Customize Views *(continued)*

5 Click Add to add the field to the view.

6 Click a field you want to remove.

7 Click Remove.

8 Click OK.

9 Click Other Settings.

10 Use the Font buttons to choose a font for Card Headings and Card Fields.

11 Enter desired card dimensions in Card Width And Multi-Line Field Height.

12 Click OK.

13 Click Automatic Formatting.

14 Click Add.

15 Type a name for the new rule.

16 Click Condition.

17 Enter your search conditions for the rule.

18 Click OK.

19 Click Font and choose a font for the new rule, then click OK.

20 Click OK.

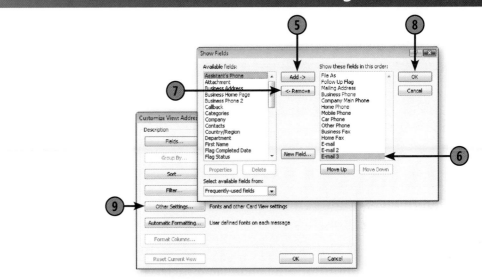

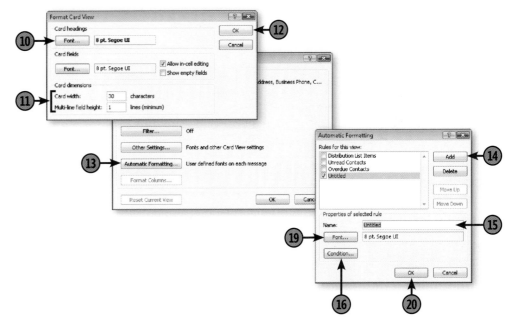

Communicating with Contacts

Microsoft Outlook makes it easy to communicate with your contacts. You can open the Contacts folder and create a new e-mail message while viewing a contact's address card, or you can use Outlook's phone dialing feature to call a contact

E-Mail a Contact

1 Click the Contacts icon on the Navigation Pane.

2 Click a contact.

3 Choose Create from the Actions menu, then choose New Message To Contact from the submenu.

4 Type a subject in the Subject field.

5 Type your message.

6 Click Send.

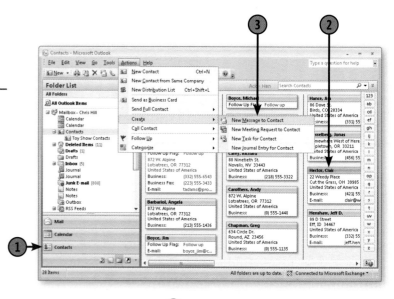

Tip

To send a message to multiple contacts, press Ctrl as you click contact names in the Contact folder. Then choose New Message To Contact from the Create submenu.

Caution

If you select a contact that does not have an e-mail address, you will receive an error message that the selected contact does not have an e-mail address or that another problem exists. You can click OK to continue, but you will not be able to send the message to that contact until you provide a valid e-mail address.

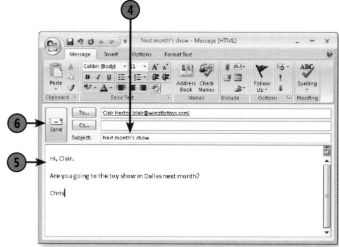

Telephone a Contact

① Click the Contacts icon on the Navigation Pane.

② Click the contact you want to call.

③ Click the Dial button on the Standard toolbar.

④ Click Start Call in the New Call dialog box. When prompted, pick up your telephone handset when the other phone begins to ring and click Talk.

⑤ Click End Call when finished.

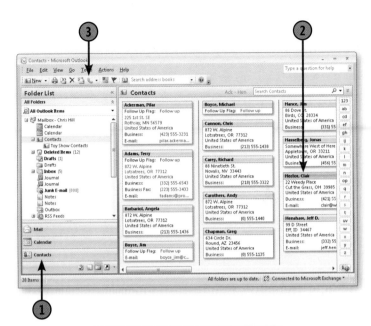

Tip

Clicking the Dial button initiates a call using the Business phone number. To use a personal number, click the arrow beside the Call button and choose the home phone. Note that if the contact has no phone information entered, the New Call dialog box will have no phone numbers available.

Tip

You can have Outlook keep a Journal entry for the phone call by selecting Create New Journal Entry When Starting New Call. This is handy if you need to track call information, including who you call, when you make the call, and the length of time the call takes.

Tip

You must have a telephone or headset connected to your modem, or the modem and phone must share the same line, for the AutoDialer option to work.

Try This!

You can modify a contact from the New Call dialog box. Click Open Contact to display the contact's address card. Edit the card as necessary, then click Save & Close.

Scheduling Meetings and Tasks for a Contact

The Contacts folder provides tools to let you schedule meetings and assign tasks to contacts. Meetings are appointments you invite others to and schedule resources for, such as meeting rooms and overhead projectors. With Outlook, you can select the contacts that you want to invite to a meeting and then let Outlook send messages to them inviting them to the meeting. You also can set up appointments with a contact in the same way, including recurring appointments that occur at the same time every day, week, month, or quarter.

Request a Meeting with a Contact

1. Click the Contacts icon in the Navigation Pane.

2. Click the contact to whom you want to send a meeting request.

3. Choose Create from the Actions menu, then choose New Meeting Request To Contact from the submenu.

(continued on the next page)

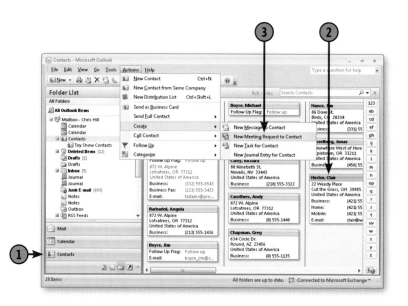

Tip

Setting up meetings and appointments for contacts works best in conjunction with Microsoft Exchange Server, but can also be used with non-Exchange accounts.

See Also

For information on managing your calendar, including appointments, see "Managing a Calendar" on page 133.

Request a Meeting with
a Contact *(continued)*

4 Type the subject of the meeting in the Subject field in the Meeting window.

5 Select or type a location in the Location drop-down list.

6 Type information about the meeting in the meeting body area.

7 Choose a start time.

8 Choose an end time.

9 Click Send.

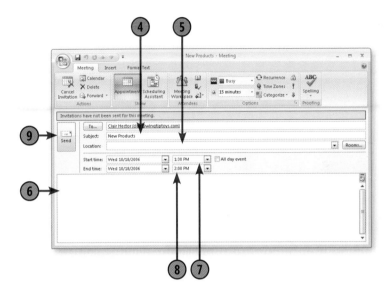

Tip

To set up a schedule for a recurring appointment, click the Recurrence button on the Standard toolbar of the Appointment window. Select the appointment time, how often the appointment should recur, and the recurrence pattern (such as "every Friday at 8 AM").

Try This!

You can set meeting reminders using the Meeting window. Select Reminder and choose a time you want the reminder to display. Click the sound icon to pick a sound file that plays when the reminder is activated.

Sharing Contact Information

As you build your contact list, you may want to share it with others in your company or among your circle of friends. Outlook enables you to share contact information by forwarding it as an Electronic Business Card, Outlook Contact item, or *vCard*. The vCard format is a standard that several e-mail clients other than Outlook support, enabling you to share contacts with others who might not have Outlook. The Electronic Business Card format is new in Outlook 2007, and provides a picture of the contact information.

Forward a Contact Item

① Click the Contacts icon in the Navigation Pane.

② Click the contact you want to share.

③ Choose Send Full Contact from the Actions menu, then choose either In Internet Format (vCard) or In Outlook Format.

④ Add an e-mail address to the message.

⑤ Type a message in the message body area.

⑥ Click Send.

See Also

For information on importing items into Outlook, see "Importing and Exporting Items" on page 222.

Tip

When the recipient receives the message with the forwarded contact item, he or she can import the information into Outlook.

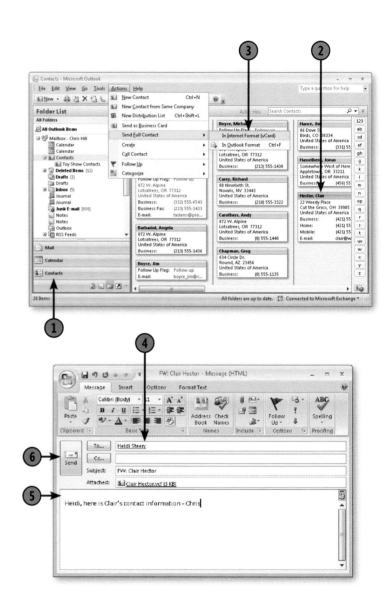

Forward a Contact Item as an Electronic Business Card

1. Click the Contacts icon in the Navigation Pane.

2. Click the contact you want to share.

3. Choose Send As Business Card from the Actions menu.

4. Add an e-mail address to the message.

5. Type a message in the message body area.

6. Click Send.

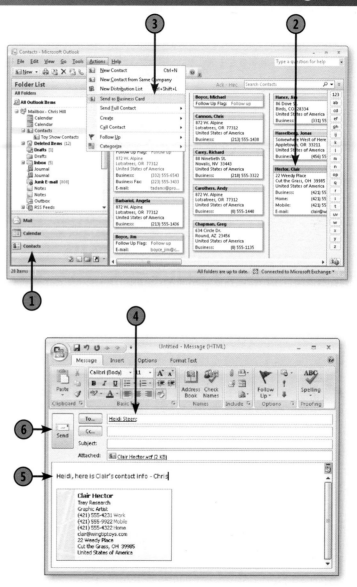

Recording Journal Entries

Outlook allows you to record Journal entries for contacts from within the Contacts folder. For example, you can create a Journal entry about a telephone conversation you had with a customer. The entry can include the name of the person you spoke with, the time it took place, the length of the call, the topic of conversation, and other information.

Log a Telephone Call

(1) Click the Contacts icon in the Navigation Pane.

(2) Click a contact.

(3) Choose Create from the Actions menu, then choose New Journal Entry For Contact from the submenu.

(4) Make any necessary changes in the Journal Entry window.

(5) Click Save & Close.

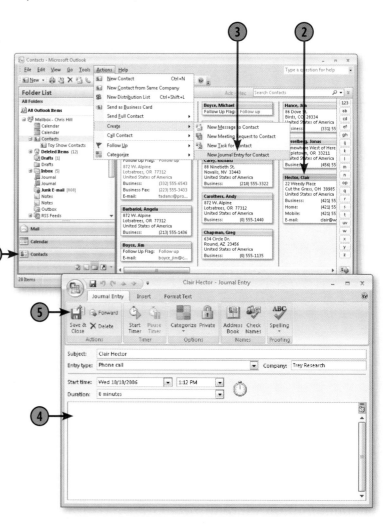

Tip

Click the Start Timer button to have Outlook keep track of when you start recording information about a person. Then click Pause Timer when you quit working with the person. Outlook keeps a running tab of the length of time you work on this contact. This is handy for anyone who must keep close track of time spent with each client or customer.

See Also

For information on using the Journal, see "Add and View Journal Items" on page 194.

8

Managing a Calendar

Microsoft Outlook's calendar simplifies the burden of keeping and maintaining a schedule of meetings, appointments, events, and tasks. At a glance, you can quickly see your agenda in daily, monthly, or yearly views. With Outlook, you won't have any excuses for missing a lunch date or forgetting a meeting.

Outlook enables you to keep track of recurring meetings or events so that you don't have to manually enter these items each time they take place. For example, you might have a weekly staff meeting that takes place every Friday from 9:00–10:00 a.m. Make it a recurring meeting, and Outlook blocks out that day and time. Similarly, if your PTA meets every third Wednesday of the month at 7:00 p.m., you can set Outlook to schedule that meeting as well.

Outlook includes a reminder alarm that displays a message prior to your Calendar items so you won't forget a meeting, appointment, or task. For example, you can set up Outlook to display a reminder of an upcoming meeting two or three days before the meeting. This way, if you need to prepare a presentation, document, or other item for the meeting you give yourself ample time to do so. You then can "snooze" the reminder so it goes off again, but perhaps only three hours prior to the meeting.

Viewing Your Calendar

With Outlook's calendar you're not stuck with one view—you can view your calendar in several different formats. Day view is an hour-by-hour view of your daily schedule, while Month view shows your schedule for the entire month. The Date Navigator is a small calendar with which you can navigate quickly to a specific day, week, or month, while the To-Do Bar consolidates all of the features of task list, Date Navigator, and appointment list into one task pane.

Use the Date Navigator

(1) Click the Calendar icon on the Navigation Pane.

(2) Click the Day tab at the top of the calendar.

(3) Click a day on the Date Navigator to display it in the Calendar view.

(4) Click to the left of a week on the Date Navigator to display that week in the Calendar view.

(5) Click the right arrow on the Date Navigator to move to the next month.

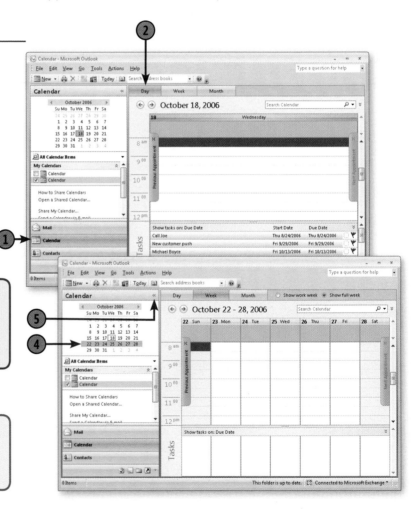

Tip

You can access the current, last three, and next three months by clicking the month name in the Date Navigator. This is handy if you want to jump back a few months or jump forward a month or two.

Try This!

To see today's date, click the Today button on the Standard toolbar. If the current month is showing in the Date Navigator, click the boxed date to display today's date.

Use the Calendar View

① Click the Calendar icon on the Navigation Pane.

② Choose a type of view from the View menu.

- ■ Click Day to see an hourly breakdown of your day.
- ■ Click Work Week to see a workweek's schedule by hour.
- ■ Click Week to see a week's schedule.
- ■ Click Month to see a month's schedule.

 Tip

You can make more room available for the Calendar pane on the screen by resizing the Navigation Pane.

 Tip

To return to today's date, right-click inside a view and choose Today from the shortcut menu that appears.

Use the To-Do Bar

① Click the Calendar icon on the Navigation Pane.

② Choose View, then choose Normal from the To-Do Bar submenu.

(continued on the next page)

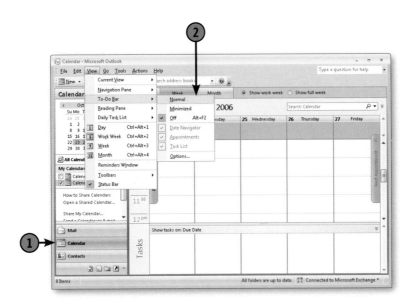

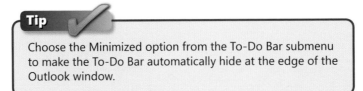

Tip

Choose the Minimized option from the To-Do Bar submenu to make the To-Do Bar automatically hide at the edge of the Outlook window.

Use the To-Do Bar *(continued)*

③ Click a date on the Date Navigator to view appointments for that date.

④ View upcoming appointments.

⑤ View current tasks.

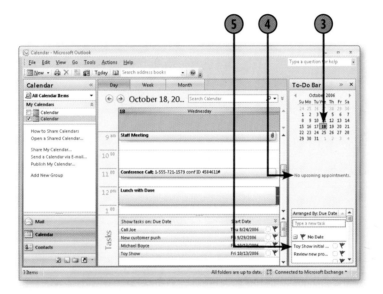

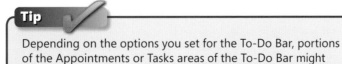

Tip

Depending on the options you set for the To-Do Bar, portions of the Appointments or Tasks areas of the To-Do Bar might be blank.

Adding an Appointment

An appointment in Outlook is an activity you enter for a specific time that, unlike a meeting, does not involve other people or resources. When you schedule an appointment, you block out a day, a time, and a location for that appoint- ment to occur. Outlook also makes it easy to set a reminder that flashes on your screen and plays a sound to alert you to the appointment.

Add an Appointment with the Menu

① Click the Calendar icon on the Navigation Pane.

② Choose New from the File menu.

③ Choose Appointment from the New submenu.

(continued on the next page)

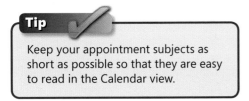

Tip

Keep your appointment subjects as short as possible so that they are easy to read in the Calendar view.

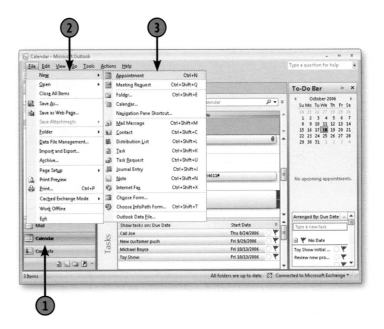

Add an Appointment with the Menu *(continued)*

④ Type a description of the appointment in the Subject box.

⑤ Type the location of the appointment in the Location box.

⑥ Click the down arrow to the right of the Start Time date, and select the day of the appointment.

⑦ Click the down arrow to the right of the Start Time hour, and select the starting time of the appointment.

⑧ Click the down arrow to the right of the End Time date, and select the ending day of the appointment if it is a multiple-day appointment.

⑨ Click the down arrow to the right of the End Time hour, and select the ending time of the appointment.

⑩ Click Save & Close.

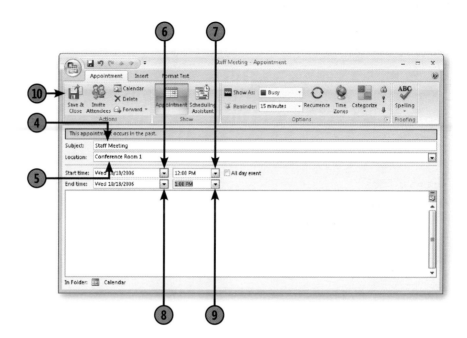

Try This!

If you'd like to add extended information about an appointment, click in the text area at the bottom of the Appointment window. Type a longer description here, such as directions to the appointment location, important information about the appointment, and so on.

Tip

You can print your appointments to the default printer by clicking the Print button on the Standard toolbar.

Add an Appointment Right on the Calendar

1. Click the Calendar icon on the Navigation pane.

2. Click and drag to select a block of time for the appointment on the Calendar.

3. Begin typing the Subject of the appointment, and the subject appears in the blocked-out space on the Calendar.

4. Press Enter.

5. Double-click the appointment to open the appointment form.

6. Add the location, notes, and other information to the appointment.

7. Click Save & Close.

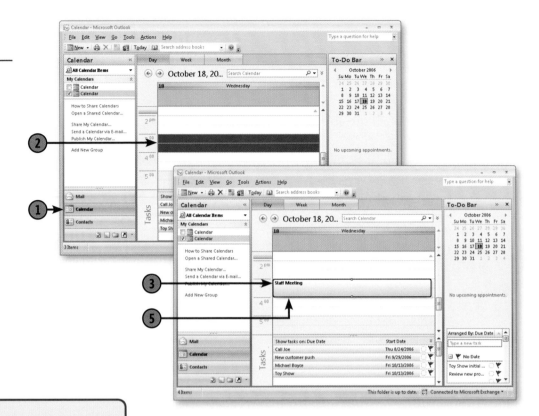

Tip

If you use Outlook on a network running Microsoft Exchange Server, you can share your appointment information with other users. This way they know when you're busy and can schedule meetings with you based on this information.

Tip

To categorize the appointment, right-click the appointment and choose Categorize, then choose a category from the submenu.

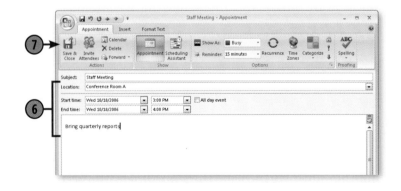

Adding an Event

An event is an activity that runs for 24 hours or longer. An example of an event is a weeklong conference or seminar you attend. Events display as banners at the top of the day and run from midnight to midnight, so they do not take up blocks of time on the Calendar. This allows you to schedule appointments or meetings during the day.

Describe the Event

1. Click the Calendar icon on the Navigation Pane.

2. Right-click on the Calendar view.

3. Choose New All Day Event from the shortcut menu.

4. Type a description of the event in the Subject box.

5. Type the location of the event in the Location box.

6. Click Save & Close

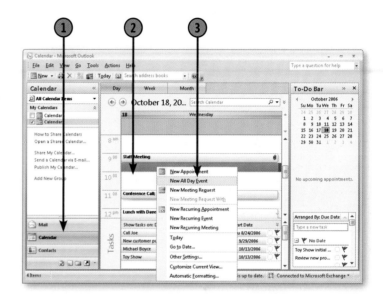

Tip

To add an all-day event to a day other than the current day, display the week or month and right-click on the day, then choose New All Day Event.

Try This!

You can add more information about an event to the text area at the bottom of the Event window.

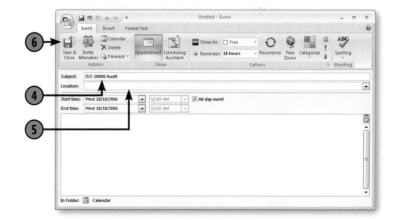

Change the Event's Scheduled Date

1 Create a new event.

2 Add a subject and location for the event.

3 Click the Start Time date down arrow and select the starting day of the event.

4 Click the End Time date down arrow and select the ending day of the event if it is a multiple-day event.

5 Click Save & Close.

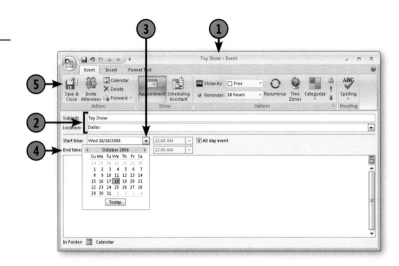

Tip

You may already have events entered in your Calendar folder. When you create a new contact in the Contacts folder and include a birthday or anniversary for the contact, Outlook schedules that date as an event in the calendar.

See Also

For information on setting up contacts, see "Working with Contacts" on page 105.

Setting Up a Meeting

A meeting is an activity that involves other people and some-times resources. A resource can be a conference room, VCR, slide projector, conference call equipment, laptop computer, or other equipment. Usually a meeting involves you and at least two other people (but can certainly be just you and one other person). Outlook sends a meeting invitation to every person you designate, and they have the option of accepting or rejecting the request, or even proposing a new time for the meeting.

Create a Meeting in a Block of Time

① Click the Calendar icon on the Navigation Pane.

② Highlight a block of time on the meeting day for the meeting.

③ Choose New Meeting Request from the Actions menu.

④ Click To.

⑤ Select attendees and resources from the Address Book, or type addresses manually.

⑥ Click OK when you are done.

⑦ Type a description of the meeting in the Subject box.

⑧ Type the location of the meeting in the Location box.

⑨ Add notes, directions, or comments for the meeting as needed.

⑩ Click Send.

Tip

If you're on a network and want to use the Meeting Planner to set up a meeting and its resources, choose Plan A Meeting from the Actions menu. Add attendees to the All Attendees list by typing them or clicking the Add Others button and selecting names from your Address Book.

Try This!

When you type your meeting subject, keep it short but descriptive. "Team Meeting" may not be enough if people are members of multiple teams. Use something specific like "Development Team Meeting" for your description.

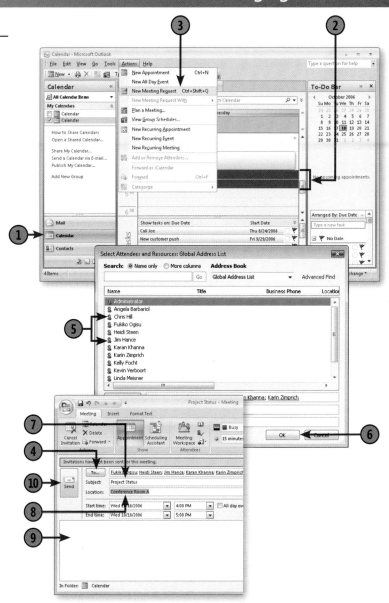

Specify a Meeting Date and Time Manually

(1) Create a new meeting.

(2) Add attendees, a subject, and a location for the meeting.

(3) Click the down arrow in the Start Time date field, and select the starting date.

(4) Click the down arrow in the Start Time hour field, and select the starting time of the meeting.

(5) Click the down arrow in the End Time hour field, and select the ending time of the meeting.

(6) Click Send.

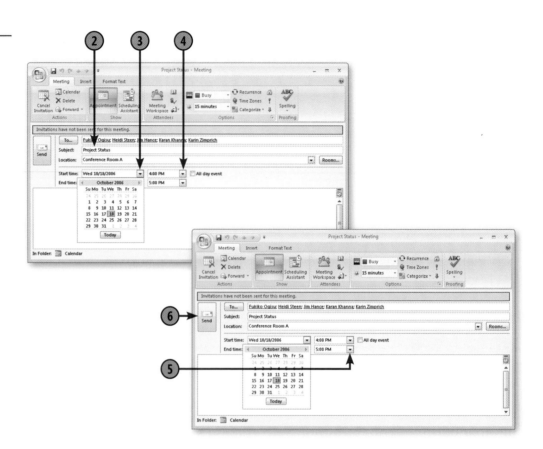

Caution

Make sure that your attendee list has correct e-mail addresses. If you attempt to send the meeting request to someone not in one of your address books, Outlook prompts you that the person cannot be validated.

See Also

For information on the Address Book and adding new contacts, see "Working with Contacts" on page 105.

Tip

Outlook provides the Meeting Planner to help you set up meetings with other people in your organization. The Meeting Planner is designed so that you can see other people's schedules if they are connected to the same local area network.

Updating Calendar Information

Outlook makes it easy to edit a meeting, appointment, or event information saved in the Calendar folder. You might, for example, need to modify the time an appointment starts or ends, change where a meeting is held, or adjust the date of an event. When you change a meeting you can send new meeting messages to attendees to announce the change.

Change an Appointment

(1) Click the Calendar icon on the Navigation Pane.

(2) Double-click the appointment you want to change (if you open a recurring appointment, Outlook asks if you want to change the occurrence or the series).

(3) Make changes to the appointment.

(4) Click Save & Close.

Tip

Any date that has a meeting, appointment, or event appears in bold on the Date Navigator. Click that date to switch to the day, week, or month in which that activity occurs.

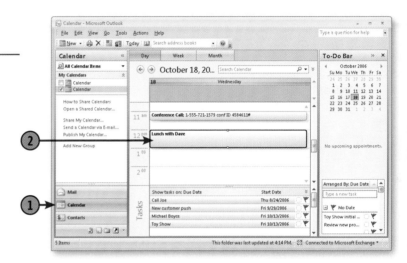

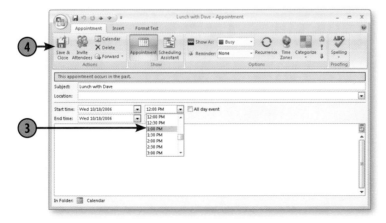

Try This!

Make an appointment recurring by clicking the Recurrence button and filling out the Appointment Recurrence information. For example, set the time for the appointment to occur from 8:00 a.m. to 10:00 a.m. every Thursday.

Update Event Information

① Click the Calendar icon on the Navigation Pane.

② Double-click the event you want to change.

③ Make changes to the event.

④ Click Save & Close.

Tip

Events appear at the top of Day and Week views and are shown within a box in Month view.

Caution

If you deselect the All Day Event option on the Appointment tab for the event, you may create a conflict with appointments or meetings you've already set up for that day. Remember that events run for 24 hours—from midnight to midnight.

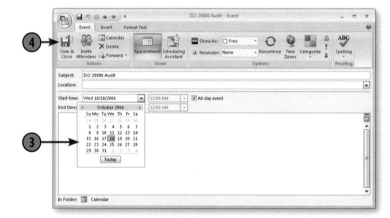

Reschedule a Meeting

① Open the meeting you want to change.

② Change the start day, if needed.

③ Click the Start Time hour drop-down list, and select the new start time.

④ Click the End Time hour drop-down list, and select the new end time.

⑤ Click Send Update.

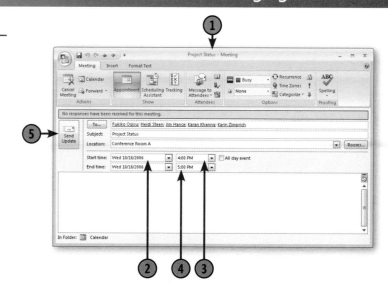

Tip

You can reschedule a meeting simply by dragging it to a new location on the Calendar. Regardless of the method you use to move the meeting, Outlook can automatically send an update to all attendees with notice of the new day and time.

Tip

Use the Tracking tab to see which attendees have responded to your meeting request.

Inserting Items, Objects, and Files in a Calendar Item

Outlook enables you to insert Outlook items, objects, and files into your Calendar items. For example, you may have a meeting to which you want to take an important document. You can insert the document into the meeting item so that you don't forget to take it with you and so that other attendees have a copy of it. Similarly, you can add Outlook items like contacts to a calendar item.

Add an Outlook Item

① Open an appointment, meeting, or event.

② Click the Insert tab on the ribbon.

③ Click Attach Item.

④ From the Look In list, select the Outlook folder in which the item is stored.

⑤ Select the Outlook item you want to insert from the Items list.

⑥ Click OK.

⑦ The selected item now appears in the comment field.

⑧ Click the Meeting, Appointment, or Event tab, and then click Save & Close.

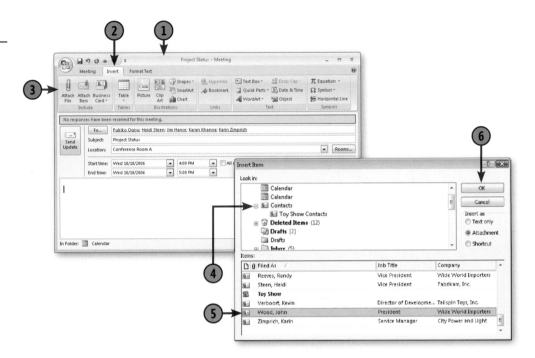

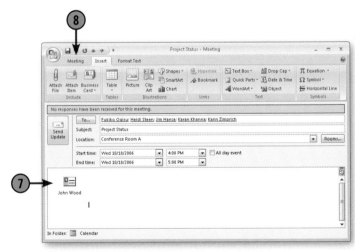

Tip ✓

Outlook uses an item-specific icon to indicate the type of Outlook item inserted, such as a note icon for a note item or calendar icon for a calendar item.

Try This!

To insert the text contained in a contact rather than the contact address card itself, select the Text Only option in the Insert Item dialog box.

Add a File

1. Double-click an appointment, meeting, or event.

2. Click the Insert tab on the ribbon.

3. Click the down arrow beside the Attach File button and choose File from the submenu.

4. Select the file you want to insert.

5. Click Insert.

6. The added file appears in the comment field.

7. Click the Meeting, Appointment, or Event tab, and then click Save & Close (or Send Update, if a meeting).

Tip

To delete a file, item, or object from a Calendar item, select the item and press Delete.

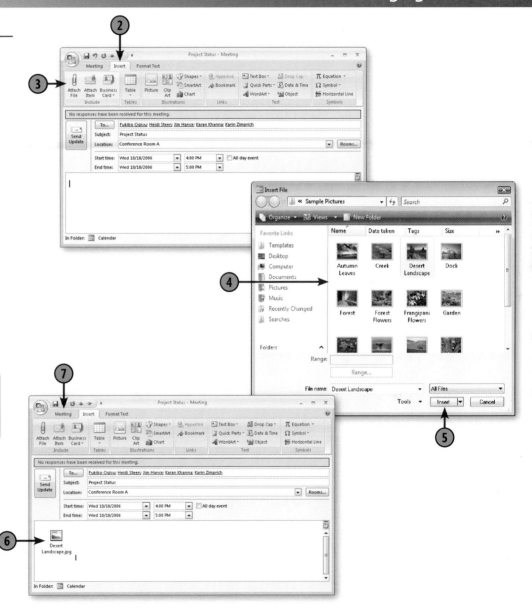

Add an Object from a File

1. Click the Calendar icon on the Navigation Pane.

2. Double-click an appointment, meeting, or event.

3. Click the Insert tab on the ribbon.

4. Click Object on the Text group of the ribbon's Insert tab.

5. Click the Create From File tab.

6. Click Browse.

(continued on the next page)

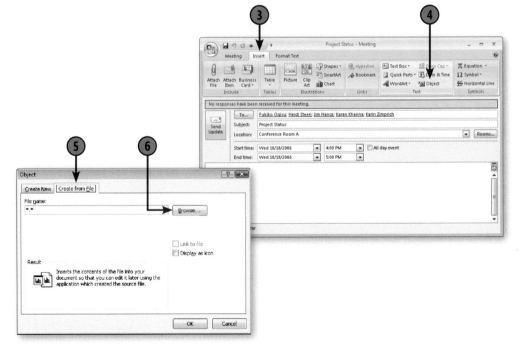

Tip

The capability to add objects from a file enables you to embed a portion of a spreadsheet or other type of document in the appointment item for reference. For example, if you are discussing a project issue list in a meeting, you might embed the issue list from an Excel spreadsheet in the meeting request so the participants can review it before the meeting.

Add an Object from
a File *(continued)*

⑦ In the dialog box, click the object you wish to add.

⑧ Click Insert, then click OK in the Object dialog box.

⑨ The added object appears in the comment field.

⑩ Click the Appointment, Meeting, or Event tab, and then click Save & Close.

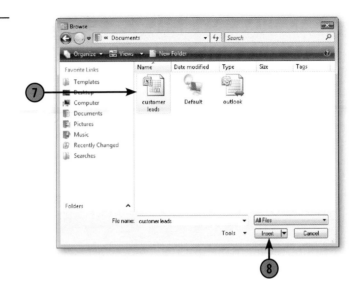

 Tip

For a meeting, click Send to send an update after you modify an existing meeting item on your Calendar.

Tip

To create a new object, such as a Microsoft Excel worksheet, when you insert it select Create New in the Insert Object dialog box. When you click OK to insert the object, you then create the new object in that object's native application (such as Microsoft Excel).

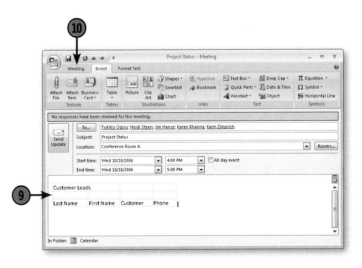

Working with Reminders

You can have Outlook display a reminder of upcoming appointments, events, or meetings. The reminder displays in a message box and can sound an alarm to alert you. You can use any sound included with Windows or use a sound that you've downloaded from the Internet and saved to your hard drive.

Tip ✓

You can set up reminders for meetings and events by following the same sequence of steps shown here for appointments.

Add or Change a Reminder

① Open the appointment, meeting, or event for which you want to set a reminder.

② In the Options group on the ribbon's Appointment tab, choose a reminder time.

③ Click Save & Close. You will be reminded of the appointment at the scheduled time.

Tip ✓

Reminders display even if the Calendar item is overdue. For example, if an event was set for Saturday and you didn't turn on your computer that day, the next time you start Windows the reminder for that event appears. You can dismiss the reminder at that point.

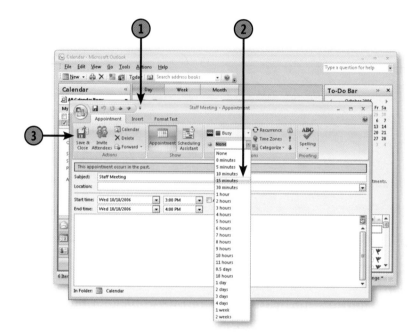

Sharing Calendar Information

Outlook enables you to share Calendar information with others. You can forward a Calendar item by e-mail to other Outlook users, or you can forward an iCalendar to any user over the Internet. You should use iCalendar when you schedule meetings with people who do not use Outlook.

Forward a Calendar Item

1 Open an existing meeting item.

2 Click the Meeting tab of the ribbon.

3 Click the Forward button.

4 Type the e-mail address of the recipient in the To box.

5 Click Send.

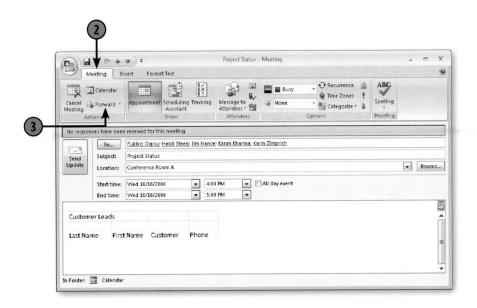

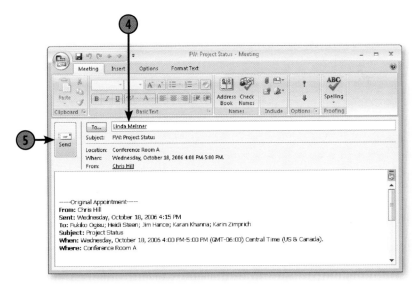

Forward an Item as an iCalendar

① Open a meeting item by double-clicking it in the Calendar.

② Click the Meeting tab on the ribbon.

③ Click the arrow beside the Forward button and choose Forward as iCalendar.

④ Type the e-mail address of the recipient in the To box.

⑤ Click Send.

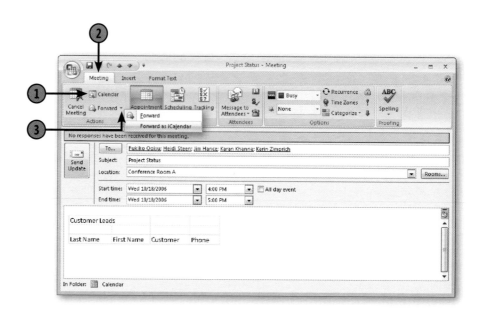

Tip

If you forward a calendar item that has an attachment, that attachment is forwarded along with the calendar item.

Tip

iCalendar is for communicating with people who do not use Outlook. If you want to forward a Calendar item to someone who uses Outlook, use the Forward command on the Actions menu or click Forward in the Actions group on the meeting form's ribbon.

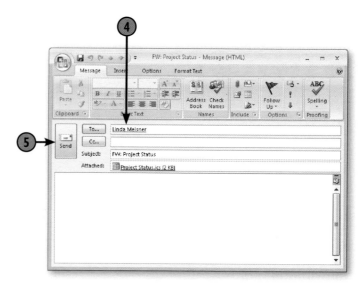

Printing Calendars

Outlook makes it easy to print your calendars. You can print your appointment calendar, such as your daily or weekly appointments, meetings, and events. Or you can print an individual calendar item, such as a meeting item.

Print your Appointment Calendar

① Click the Calendar icon on the Navigation Pane.

② Choose Print from the File menu.

③ Choose a calendar view in the Print Style area.

④ Click OK.

Tip

You can print your calendars in daily, weekly, monthly, tri-fold, calendar detail, and memo style. Print your calendar in each one of these styles and pick your favorite one.

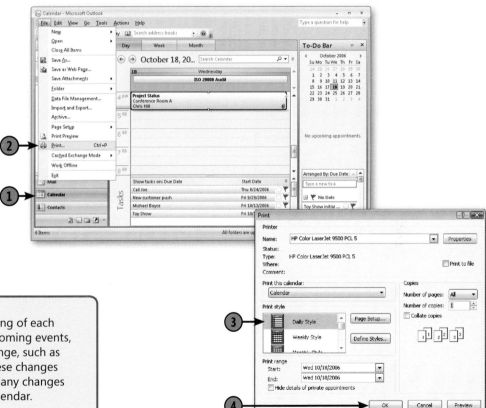

Try This!

Print your appointment calendar at the beginning of each week so that you can keep track of all your upcoming events, appointments, and meetings. As schedules change, such as a meeting being delayed or canceled, make these changes on the hard copy as well as in Outlook. If too many changes happen, of course, you need to print a fresh calendar.

Print a Calendar Item

① Click the Calendar icon on the Navigation Pane.

② Double-click the Calendar item you want to print.

③ Click the Microsoft Office button and choose Print from the File menu.

④ Set print options.

⑤ Click OK.

Tip

If you want to print to a printer other than the default one, click the Name drop-down list and select the printer.

Try This!

Print a Calendar item that has an attachment inserted in it. When the Print dialog box appears, select Print Attached Files to print the attachment.

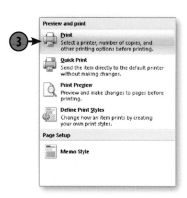

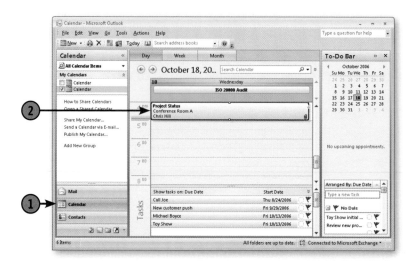

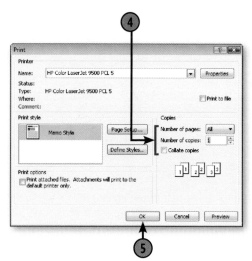

9

Working with Tasks

Most of us at some time or another have written a to-do list—a list of tasks we need to perform. Maybe you put together a list of the improvements or repairs you want to make to your house. Maybe it is something simpler like a list of errands to run. Whatever the case, having a list of the tasks you need to complete can be valuable for keeping you on track.

Microsoft Office Outlook 2007 includes a feature to help you stay on track. The Tasks folder stores your to-do list. You can create tasks for yourself, assign them a due date, and easily mark them as completed. You can create one-time tasks or recurring tasks. Outlook also lets you assign tasks to others and receive status updates on the tasks from the people to whom you assign them. This section explains how to use the Tasks folder to create and manage one-time and recurring tasks, as well as assign tasks to others.

Viewing Your Tasks

Outlook includes a Tasks folder that you can use to store your tasks and tasks that you assign to others. The Tasks folder offers a handful of ways to view and work with your tasks, including the Daily Task List that appears at the bottom of the Calendar, and the Tasks List in the To-Do Bar. The default view for the Tasks folder is the Simple List view, which shows whether the task is complete, the name (subject) of the task, and the due date.

Open the Task Item Window

1. Click the Tasks icon on the Navigation Pane to open the Tasks folder.

2. Double-click a task to open the task's form. If you don't have a task created yet, just double-click in the Tasks folder to start a new task.

3. Click Details in the Show group of the ribbon's Task tab to display additional task information.

4. Click Save & Close to close the form.

Tip

You can easily change views in the Tasks folder. Just click a view in the Navigation Pane, or choose Current View from the View menu, then choose a view from the cascading menu.

Tip

When you create a task, Outlook doesn't set up a reminder for the task, but you can add one later. Open the task, click the Task tab, select the Reminder checkbox, and then select the date and time for the reminder from the two drop-down lists beside the Reminder checkbox.

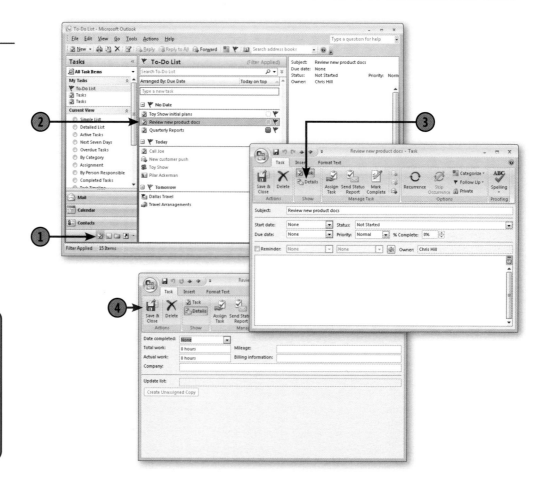

Use the Task List

1 In Outlook, click the Tasks icon on the Navigation Pane to open the Tasks folder.

2 When the Tasks folder opens, click the Arranged By column and choose an item by which to sort the list.

3 Click Arranged By again, and click Due Date to restore the default sort method.

4 Click the flag beside the task's subject to mark the task as complete.

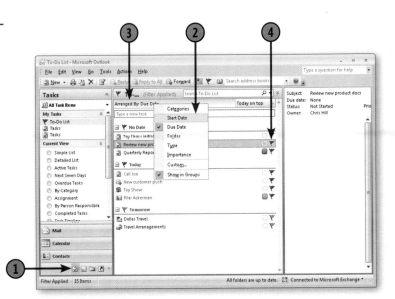

Tip

You can add and remove columns from the Task List to show the task data most important to you. Right-click the column header and select Field Chooser. In the Field Chooser dialog box, click a column and drag it to the column header. To remove a column, drag it from the column header to the Field Chooser dialog box. Note that you must widen some views or turn off the Reading Pane to accomplish this with some views (such as the To-Do List).

Tip

If you don't see the To-Do List, click To-Do List in the Navigation Pane.

Use the Task List in the Calendar

① Click the Calendar icon on the Navigation Pane to open the Calendar folder.

② Click the Day or Week tab.

③ View the tasks in the Task List.

④ Click the flag beside a task to mark it as complete.

⑤ Choose Undo Flag from the Edit menu to restore the task to the list.

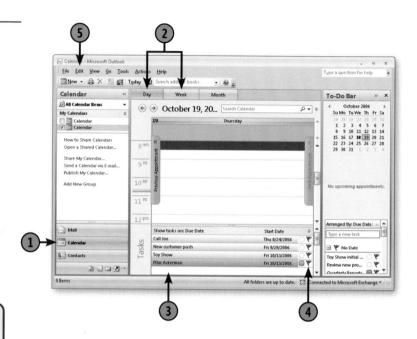

Tip

If you can't see the Daily Task List, choose Daily Task List from the View menu, then choose Normal.

Tip

The Outlook Today view includes a simplified task list that shows the subject and completion status. You can click on a task's subject to open the task to view its details or modify it. Click the checkbox beside a task to mark it as complete.

See Also

The Outlook Today view is built using HTML, the same language used to design Web pages. If you have some knowledge of HTML, you can create a custom Outlook Today view. See *Microsoft Office Outlook 2007 Inside Out* (Redmond, WA: Microsoft Press, 2007).

Adding a Task

Tasks can be added to your Tasks folder in one of two ways: You can create the task yourself or accept a task that someone else assigns to you. If you create the task yourself, you can create it by using the New menu, or you can create it through the Tasks folder.

Set the Task Name and Due Date

① Click the Tasks icon on the Navigation Pane to open the Tasks folder.

② Click New to start a new task.

③ Type a subject for the task.

④ Click the arrow beside the Due Date field and select a date from the date navigator.

⑤ Click Save & Close.

Tip

With any folder open, you can use the New menu to open a new task form and create the task. Click the arrow beside the New button on the Standard toolbar and choose Task from the submenu to open the new task form.

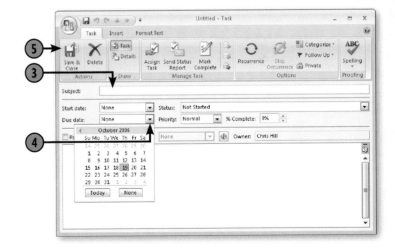

Set or Change Task Properties

① Click the Tasks icon on the Navigation Pane to open the Tasks folder.

② Double-click the task whose properties you want to change to open the task form.

③ Click the Task tab.

④ Modify the start and end dates, if needed.

⑤ Click the Status drop-down list and choose a status, such as Started, In Progress, or Completed.

⑥ Select a priority from the Priority drop-down list.

⑦ Specify the percent complete in the % Complete field.

⑧ Click the Details button.

(continued on the next page)

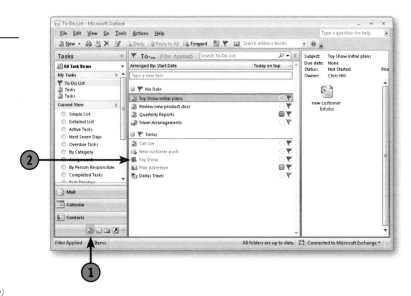

Tip

Outlook makes a connection between the Status and % Complete properties. If you specify some percentage less than 100% in the % Complete field, Outlook changes the Status field to In Progress. Setting % Complete to 100% causes Outlook to set Status to Completed. Likewise, setting Status to Completed sets % Complete to 100%.

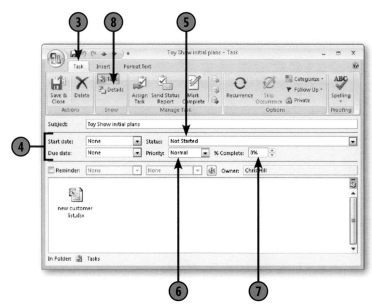

Set or Change Task Properties *(continued)*

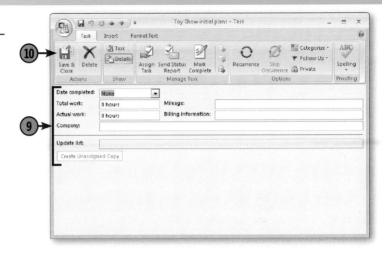

(9) Set additional properties for the task.

(10) Click Save & Close to close the form.

Try This!

If you delegate an Outlook folder to other users, allowing them to open your folder and view the items in it, they can see all items not marked private. Use the Private button in the Options group of the ribbon's Task tab to prevent your delegates from seeing the task in your task list.

Tip

When you set a reminder for a task, Outlook doesn't assign a sound for the reminder—it only displays the reminder in the Reminders dialog box when the specified time arrives. You can click the Speaker button next to the Reminder date and time fields to select a sound file for Outlook to play when it displays the reminder.

See Also

For more information on working with reminders, see "Working with Reminders" on page 152.

Working with Recurring Tasks

Some tasks are recurring tasks—they repeat on a regular basis. For example, maybe you have to prepare a set of reports every Friday that summarizes the week's sales or other information. Or perhaps you need to back up your files every week. Although a recurring task shows up only once in the task list, it appears in the Tasks lists in the Calendar and on the To-Do Bar when the assigned due date falls in the list's range. If you set a reminder for the task, you receive the reminder for each recurrence of the task.

Create a Recurring Task

(1) Click the Tasks icon on the Navigation Pane to open the Tasks folder.

(2) Click New on the Standard toolbar to open a form for the new task.

(3) Set the Subject, Due Date, and other information for the task.

(4) Click Recurrence in the Options group of the ribbon's Task tab to open the Task Recurrence dialog box.

(continued on the next page)

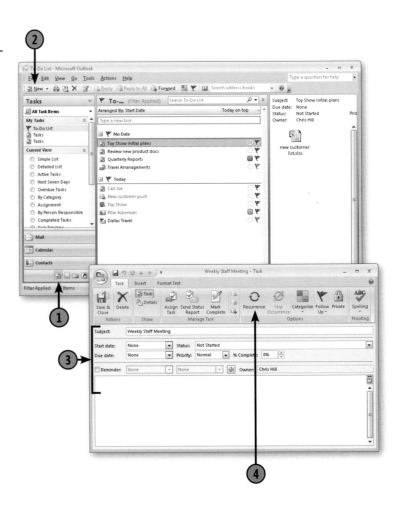

Tip

If you set a recurring task with no end date, you can still revise the task's properties to make it end after a specified number of occurrences or specified date. Just open the task's properties, click Recurrence to open the Task Recurrence dialog box, choose the desired end option, and click OK. Then click Save & Close to save the changes.

Create a Recurring Task *(continued)*

⑤ Select the type of recurrence.

⑥ Specify how often the task should recur, or specify that Outlook should create the new task after the current one is complete.

⑦ Set the start and end of the recurrence period.

⑧ Click OK.

⑨ Click Save & Close to close the task's form.

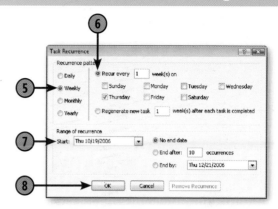

Tip

Select the Recur Every option in the Task Recurrence dialog box when you want the task to recur even if the previous occurrence hasn't been completed. Select the Regenerate New Task option if you want the task to recur only after the last occurrence is complete.

Try This!

You can make a recurring task nonrecurring by opening a task's form, clicking Recurrence on the toolbar to open the Task Recurrence dialog box, and then clicking Remove Recurrence.

Modifying and Updating a Task

You can modify a task at any time to change any property, including subject, due date, recurrence, and so on. Another change you'll want to make to tasks is to mark them as complete. This allows you to see at a glance which tasks are complete and which are not. You can also change the view of the Tasks folder to show only tasks that are complete, only tasks that are overdue, only those that are incomplete, and so on. In addition to marking tasks complete, you'll probably want to delete completed tasks and send status updates for tasks that are assigned to you.

Mark a Task as Complete

(1) Click the Tasks icon on the Navigation Pane to open the Tasks folder.

(2) Click Simple List in the Navigation Pane.

(3) Click the checkbox in the Complete column to mark a task as complete.

(4) Note that Outlook displays completed tasks using strikethrough.

Tip

You can click the checkbox next to a task on the Tasks List (Day, Week, or Work Week views in the Calendar) to mark a task as complete.

Try This!

You can mark a task complete by setting its percent complete value to 100%. Open the task and use the arrow button beside the % Complete option to set the value to 100%. Outlook marks the task as complete.

Tip

You can mark tasks complete in any task view; these steps introduce you to the Simple List view as a means for viewing all tasks as a list, as well as marking tasks complete. If your current view does not include a Complete column, you can right-click a task and choose Mark Complete.

Delete a Completed Task

 Select the task in any folder where the task is visible.

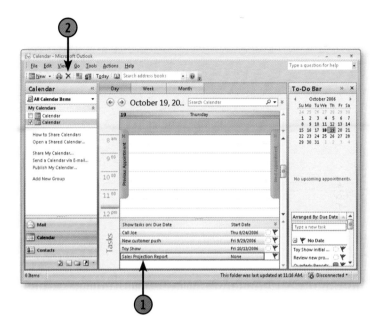 Click the Delete button on the Standard toolbar to delete the task.

Tip

You can delete any task, whether or not the task is marked as complete. Use the same method to delete an incomplete task that you use to delete a complete task.

Tip

When you delete a task, Outlook places the task in the Deleted Items folder. If you delete the wrong task or decide you don't want to delete it after all, you can restore it to the Tasks folder. Using the Folder List in the Navigation Pane, open the Deleted Items folder and drag the task to the Tasks icon. You can also right-click a task in the Deleted Items folder, choose Move To Folder, select the Tasks folder, and click OK to move it back.

Send a Status Report for an Assigned Task

① Click the Tasks icon on the Navigation Pane to open the Tasks folder.

② Double-click the task to open its form.

③ Make changes to the task's properties as needed.

④ Click the Save button to save the changes.

⑤ Click Send Status Report in the Manage Task group of the ribbon's Task tab.

(continued on the next page)

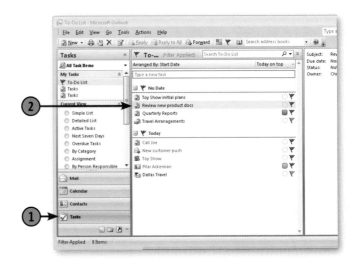

Try This!

You can send a copy of a status report to a person not on the update list without letting the people on the list know that you've copied that person. Just use the Bcc field to address the message to the other person. If Outlook isn't currently showing the Bcc field, choose Show Bcc from the Fields group under the Options tab.

See Also

For more information on assigning tasks to others, see "Assigning a Task to Someone Else" on page 174.

See Also

For more information on adding and editing text in a message form, see "Changing Message Text" on page 56.

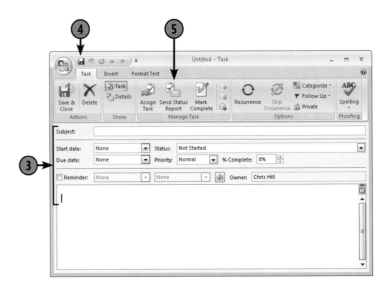

Send a Status Report for an Assigned Task *(continued)*

⑥ Outlook adds the update address list (person who assigned the task to you); click To or Cc to add addresses for people not included in the update list.

⑦ Click in the body of the message and add notes or comments as desired.

⑧ Click Send to send the message.

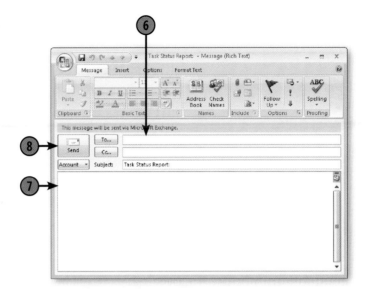

Tip

Outlook fills in the status information in the body of the update message for you. You can edit this text if needed. Just highlight the text you want to change, and type the replacement text.

See Also

For more information on addressing e-mail messages and working with the address book, see "Writing an E-Mail Message" on page 48.

Inserting Items into a Task

When you create a task—whether you create the task for yourself or assign it to someone else—you might want to add items to the task. For example, assume you're going to assign a task to someone else, and that person needs a copy of a Word document to perform the task. You can attach the document to the task. Or perhaps you need to include some contacts with a task. Whatever the case, it's easy to insert Outlook items, objects, and files in a task.

Add an Outlook item

1. Click the Tasks icon on the Navigation Pane to open the Tasks folder.

2. Double-click a task to open its form.

3. Click the Insert tab on the ribbon.

4. Click in the notes area of the Task.

5. In the Include group, click Attach Item. *(continued on the next page)*

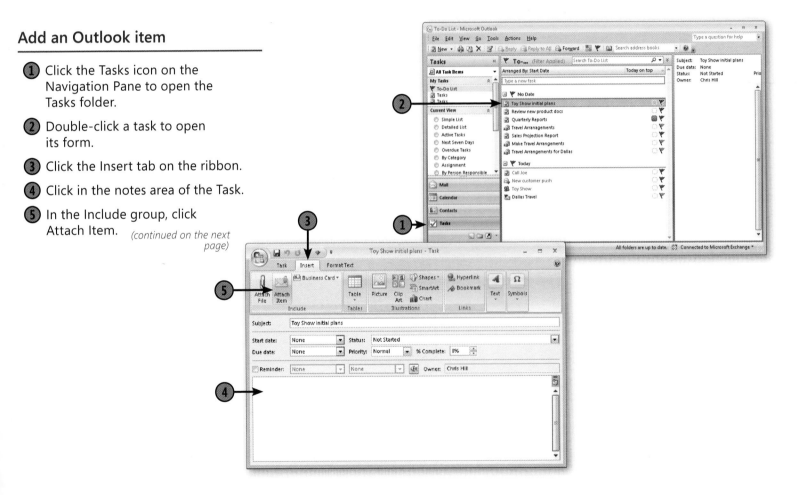

Add an Outlook item *(continued)*

6 Select the Outlook folder containing the object you want to insert.

7 Select the item to insert.

8 Select an option to specify how the object will be inserted.

9 Click OK.

10 Click Task, and then click Save & Close.

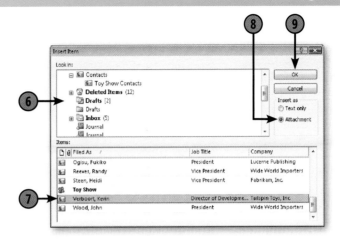

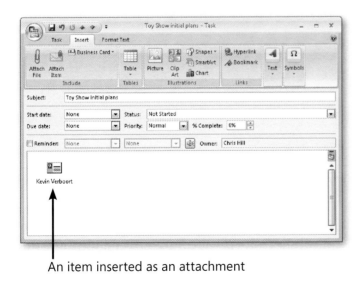

An item inserted as an attachment

An item inserted as text only

Add a File

① Click the Tasks icon to open the Tasks folder.

② Double-click a task to open its form.

③ Click the Insert tab on the ribbon.

④ Click the Attach File button in the Attach group.

(continued on the next page)

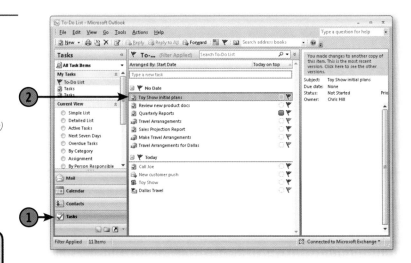

See Also

For more information about attaching files to e-mail messages rather than adding them to tasks, see "E-Mailing a File" on page 67.

Tip

When you insert a file as a hyperlink, Outlook inserts the path to the document. If you insert a file from your local computer, the path uses the local drive letter. This works fine for creating hyperlinks to documents you use, but doesn't work when assigning a tasks to other people, because clicking the link on their end causes Outlook to try to open the file from their computers. However, you can link files on network servers in tasks that you assign, as long as you view the server through a UNC path rather than a mapped drive. A UNC path has the form \\server\folder, where server is the name of the server and folder the name of the shared folder on the server where the document is located.

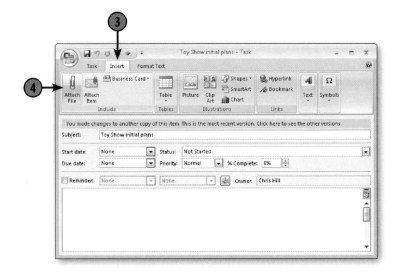

Add a File *(continued)*

⑤ Select the file you want to insert.

⑥ Click Insert to insert the file.

⑦ Outlook inserts the file as an icon in the task.

⑧ Add other information to the task as needed.

⑨ Click Task, and then click Save & Close.

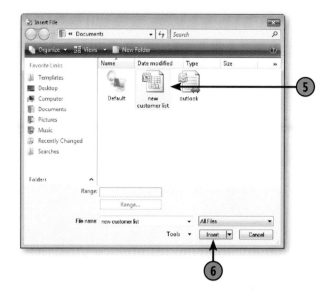

Tip

You can insert a file as a hyperlink rather than as an attachment, which allows the task to be opened from its source rather than included in the task. The main benefit to this is you don't duplicate the document but instead create a shortcut to it. The limitation is that everyone who receives the message must have access to wherever the file is stored. To insert a hyperlink in a task, open the task and click Attach File on the Insert tab. Select the file, click the arrow beside the Insert button, and then choose Insert As Hyperlink.

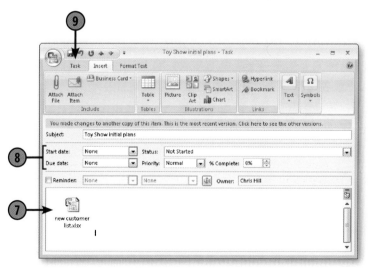

Assigning a Task to Someone Else

If you manage others and use Outlook in your organization for e-mail and collaboration, you'll probably want to assign tasks to others. Outlook sends the task assignment as an e-mail message and the assignee has the option of accepting or rejecting the task. When you assign a task you define a status update distribution list. The people on that list receive status reports when the assignee makes changes to the task.

Assign a Task

1. Click the arrow beside New on the Standard toolbar and choose Task Request to open a new task form that includes message address fields.

(continued on the next page)

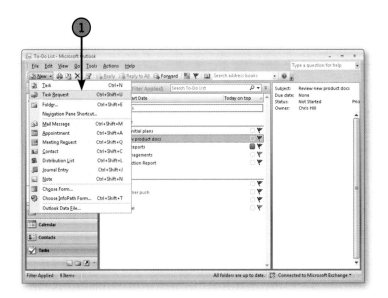

Try This!

If you want to pass the buck and reassign a task that was assigned to you to someone else, accept the task, open the task, click Assign Task in the Manage Task group of the ribbon's Task tab, and assign it by typing someone's name or selecting a name from your address list.

See Also

For information on how to include a document with a task you assign to someone else, see "Inserting Items into a Task" on page 170.

Tip

When you assign a task to another person, a copy of the task request message goes into your Sent Items folder. If you open the message, its form shows a status message indicating that Outlook is waiting for a response from the assignee. This message changes after the assignee either accepts or rejects the task.

Assign a Task *(continued)*

② Use the fields on the Task tab to define the task.

③ Select Keep An Updated Copy Of This Task On My Task List to have Outlook keep track of the assigned task with a copy on your own task list that updates as the assignee works on the task.

④ Select Send Me A Status Report When This Task Is Complete to have Outlook send you a status report when the assignee completes the task.

⑤ Type the assignee's name, or click To and select the person to whom you want to assign the task from your Contacts list.

⑥ Click the Details button.

⑦ Add other information for the task.

⑧ Click Task to return to the task form.

⑨ Click Send.

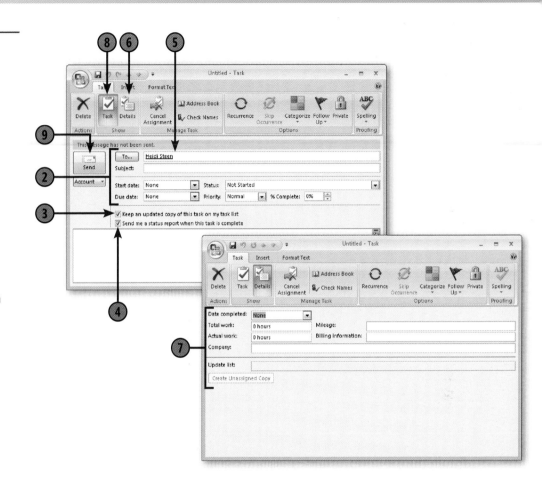

Accept or Reject an Assigned Task

① Click the Mail icon on the Navigation Pane and open the Inbox.

② Click the Task Request message to select it. If the Preview Pane is not open, double-click the message to open it.

③ Click Accept to accept the task, or Decline to decline the task.

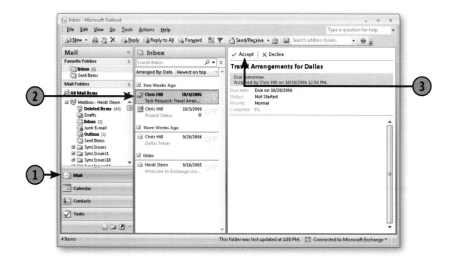

Tip

When you accept or reject a task, Outlook deletes the task request message from your Inbox. You can't control this behavior to prevent Outlook from deleting the message. However, Outlook keeps copies in your Sent Items folder of task requests that you create.

Tip

When you reassign a task that someone has assigned to you and that third person accepts the task, Outlook sends an acceptance notice to you and to the task's originator. The status update list then includes the originator's address and yours, so you receive status updates along with the originator.

Sharing Task Information

Sometimes you might need to share a task with someone else. For example, you might need to include information about a task in a written report. Or perhaps you need to print a list of tasks to include in an information packet for a staff meeting. Outlook gives you several ways to share tasks, including printing them and sending them through e-mail messages.

Print a Task List

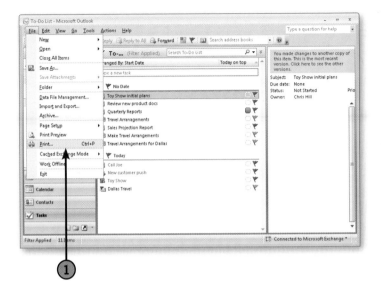

(1) Open the Tasks folder and choose Print from the File menu.

(2) In the Print dialog box, choose the printer to which you want to print the list.

(3) Select Table Style from the Print Style menu.

(4) Click OK to print the list.

Try This!

Sometimes you might not want to include all of your tasks in the printed list. Open the Tasks folder, hold down the Ctrl key, and click on the tasks you want included in the list. Choose Print from the File menu, select the printer, and then select Only Selected Rows. Click OK to print the selected tasks.

See Also

For more information on printing your schedule, see "Printing Calendars" on page 155.

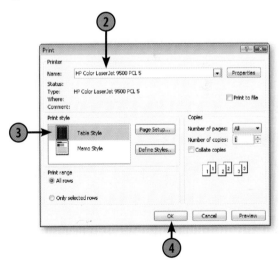

Print a Task Item

① Open the Tasks folder and open the task you want to print.

② Click the Microsoft Office button and choose Print.

③ Choose the number of copies you need to print.

④ Select the Print Attached Files option if you want to also print any attached files along with the task.

⑤ Click OK to print the task.

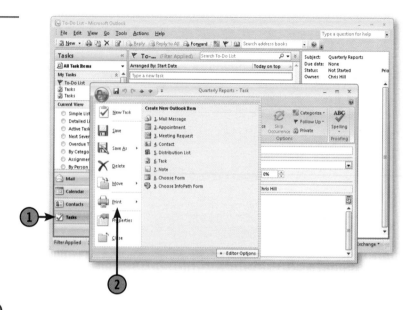

Tip

If you don't need to set any printing options but just want to quickly print a task, right-click the task in the task list and choose Print. Outlook sends the task to the printer without prompting for any other information.

See Also

For more information about attaching files to a task, see "Add a File" on page 149.

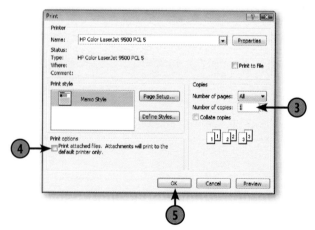

Forward a Task

① Open the Tasks folder and right-click a task.

② Choose Forward to open a message with the task as an attachment.

③ Select the recipient for the message.

④ Add notes or other comments in the body of the message.

⑤ Click Send to send the message.

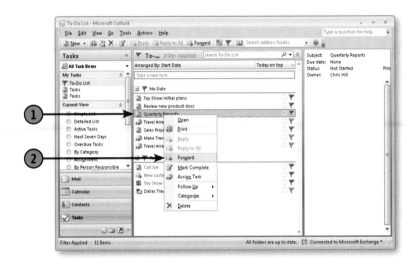

See Also

For more information on composing e-mail messages, see "Writing an E-Mail Message" on page 48.

Tip

You can forward a task from the task window as well as from the Tasks folder. With the task open, choose Forward from the Manage Task group of the Task tab.

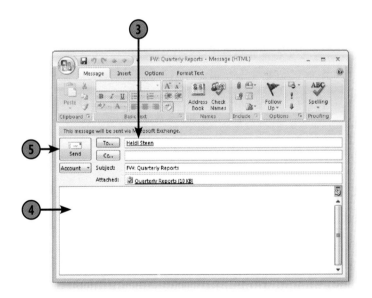

10

Working with Notes

If you're like most people, you probably have lots of notes littering your desk or stuck to your monitor, and they help you organize your day (or they would, if the notes themselves weren't so disorganized). Some of those notes are probably important enough that you'd have a hard time getting by without them.

You can get organized and clean up your desk at the same time by using Outlook to keep track of all your notes. Outlook provides a Notes folder you can use to create and view electronic notes. As with other Outlook items, you can print these notes, save them on your computer, and even stick them right on your Windows desktop.

This section explains how to work with the Notes folder in Outlook. You learn how to create and view notes, edit and delete them, and use different colors for your notes. You also learn how to cut and copy notes, print them (when you simply must have a hard copy), and attach them to e-mail messages.

Viewing Notes

As with other types of items, Outlook provides a folder specifically for working with notes. You can create additional notes folders if you like, or just work with the main Notes folder. The initial view for the Notes folder shows the notes as icons with the first few lines of the note text underneath the icon. When you click on a note to select it, Outlook shows more of the text.

Open the Notes Folder

1 Click the Notes icon on the Outlook Bar to open the Notes folder.

2 Choose Current View from the View menu, then choose Notes List. This causes the first few lines of each note to be displayed.

3 View the first few lines of the notes in the folder window.

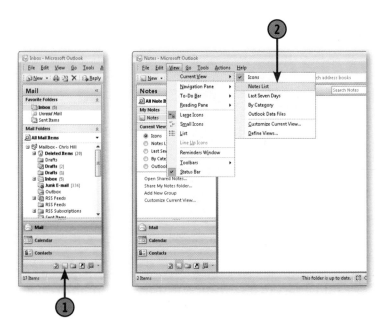

Tip

You can also simply click Notes List in the Navigation Pane to view the Notes List view.

See Also

For more information on creating other folders in Outlook for storing notes, see "Organizing with Folders" on page 211.

Tip

Outlook provides several different views of the Notes folder. Use the Last Seven Days View to see the notes that have been created or modified in the last seven days.

Read a Note

① Click the Notes icon on the Outlook Bar to open the Notes folder.

② Double-click the icon of the note you want to read to open it in a window.

③ View the time the note was last updated and saved.

④ Click and drag the window corner to resize the note window.

⑤ Click the Close button to close the note window.

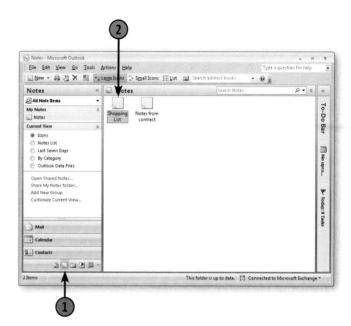

Tip

If you don't have any notes in your Notes folder, just double-click in the Notes folder and type some text to create a note.

See Also

For information on how to change the color of a note, see "Customizing the Notes Folder" on page 187.

Tip

You can click on the small note icon in the upper-left corner of the note's window to perform any of several commands on the note, such as saving it, changing its color, and more.

Creating a Note

Working with notes is one of the easiest tasks in Outlook. Notes are little more than text files, and creating a new note is as easy as creating a file with Notepad or WordPad. Outlook opens an empty window when you start a new note, ready for your text. You can easily edit a note to change its contents or add more text. Finally, when you don't need the note anymore you can simply delete it.

Add a Note

1. Click the Notes icon on the Outlook Bar to open the Notes folder.

2. Click New on the Standard toolbar to open a new note window.

3. Start typing the note text in the note window.

4. Click the Close button to save the changes and close the note window.

(continued on the next page)

Tip

To place a copy of a note on the Windows desktop, just drag it from the Notes window in Outlook and drop it on the desktop.

Tip

You can insert blank lines in a note simply by pressing Enter twice.

Try This!

To see how the note date and time feature works, start by creating a new note. Type some text and notice the date and time at the bottom of the window. Close the note and wait a few minutes. When you reopen the note you see that the time has not changed.

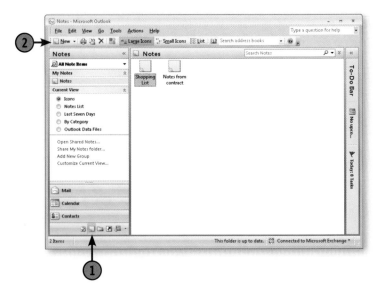

Add a Note (continued)

5 Outlook adds an icon to the Notes window for the new note.

Tip

To edit a note, just double-click on the note in the Notes folder. When the note opens, you can edit it just as you would any other text document. You are limited to keystroke short-cuts, though, because there are no buttons or menus in the note window. For instance, to copy and paste text, you will have to select the text, press Ctrl+C, move your cursor to where you want the text inserted, and press Ctrl+V. When you have finished making changes to the note, just click the Close button in the note window to close it.

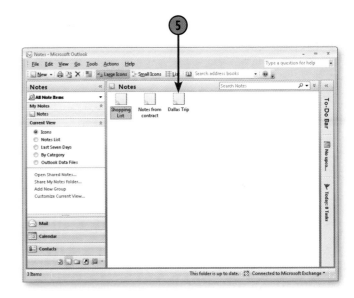

Delete a Note

1 Click the Notes icon on the Outlook Bar to open the Notes folder.

2 Click to select the note you want to delete.

3 Click the Delete button on the Standard toolbar.

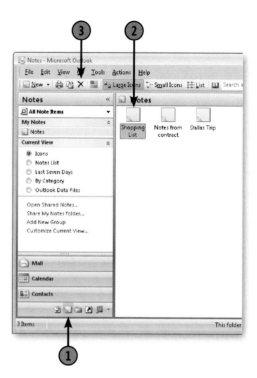

Tip

You can select a note and press Delete to delete it. You can also select more than one note and delete them all at the same time.

Tip

Hold down the Ctrl key while clicking notes to select multiple notes for deletion.

Try This!

As with other Outlook items, notes you delete are placed in the Deleted Items folder. Unless you have emptied the Deleted Items folder, you can recover the notes if needed by opening it and dragging the notes back to the Notes folder.

Customizing the Notes Folder

Unlike most other Outlook folders, the Notes folder offers only a few settings. You can change the color Outlook uses for new notes, the note font, and the initial window size for new notes. You can change the font used by all notes but not the font used by individual notes. In other words, all notes have the same font and font size. However, you can set note color individually by assigning a color category to the note.

Change Note Color

(1) Right-click a note.

(2) Choose Categorize from the menu.

(3) Select a color category for the note.

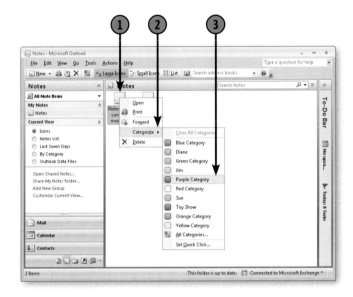

Tip

You can use color to identify other Outlook items. For example, you can specify the color used for specific types of tasks. You can also apply color to appointments in the Calendar folder to identify specific types of appointments. Color categories enable you to quickly identify items in Outlook, and you can also sort by these categories when needed.

Change the Notes Folder View

① Click Small Icons on the Standard toolbar.

② View the notes as small icons with the note text beside the icon.

③ Click Notes List in the Navigation Pane to view the notes as a list with more of the note text shown.

④ Click By Category to view notes grouped by category.

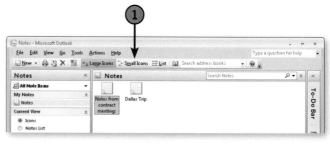

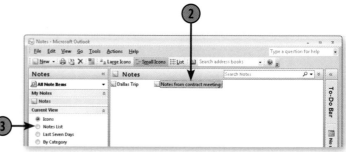

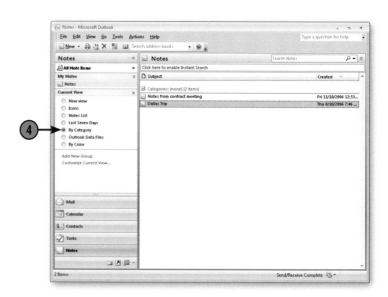

Tip

You can right-click a note and choose Categorize, then choose a category to assign the note to that category.

See Also

For more information on working with different views, see "Viewing Items and Folders" on page 42.

Tip

You're not restricted to using the notes views provided by Outlook. You can create your own views as well. Choose Current View from the View menu, then choose Define Views.

Sharing Notes

You can share notes with others in a handful of different ways, just as you can share other Outlook items. For example, you can e-mail a note to someone or print it to save a hard copy or send with a report. You can also use the Clipboard to copy notes to other Outlook items or other programs.

E-Mail a Note

(1) Open the Notes folder and select the note you want to send as e-mail.

(2) Choose Forward from the Actions menu to open a message window with the note attached to the message.

(3) Add some text, if desired.

(4) Click in the Subject field and modify the subject, if desired.

(5) Add a recipient for the message.

(6) Click Send to send the message.

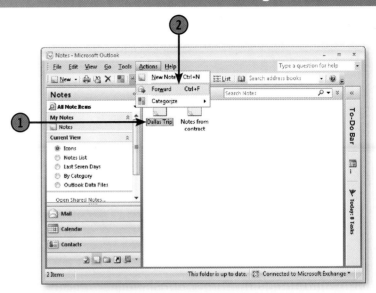

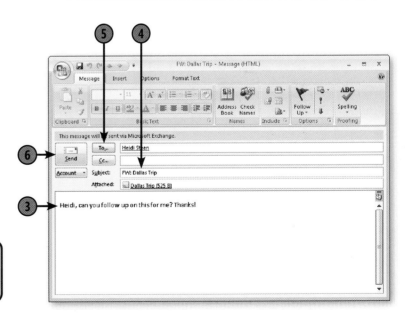

See Also

For more information on creating new e-mail messages, see "Writing an E-Mail Message" on page 48.

Print a Note

① Open the Notes folder and select the note you want to print.

② Choose Print from the File menu.

③ Specify the number of copies you want to print.

④ Click OK to print the note.

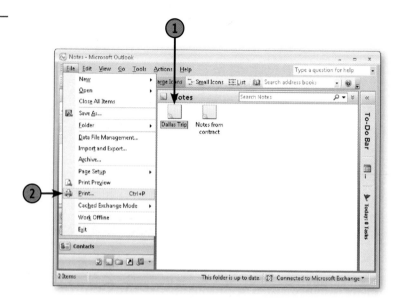

 Tip

If you right-click a note and choose Print, Outlook sends the note to your default printer without prompting you for any printing options.

Try This!

You can print more than one note at a time. Select all the notes you want to print and choose Print from the File menu, just as you would for a single note. Select the Start Each Item On A New Page option if you want to print each note on a separate page.

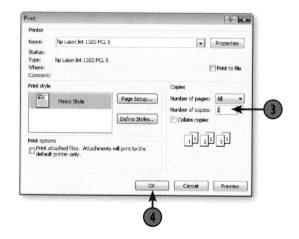

Copy or Cut a Note

1 Open the Notes folder and open the note you want to cut or copy.

2 Highlight the text in the note.

3 Press Ctrl+C to copy the text to the Clipboard.

4 Open the program or Outlook item where you want to use the note text.

5 Click Paste in the ribbon.

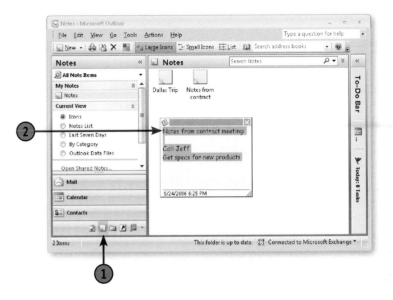

Tip

If you click a note icon and choose Copy from the Edit menu or press Ctrl+C, the note is placed on the Clipboard as an object, not as text.

Tip

When you cut a note, Outlook removes all the text from the note, but doesn't delete the blank note from the Notes folder. To delete the note, select it and click Delete.

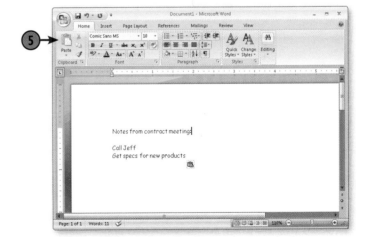

Using the Journal

The Journal is another important feature in Microsoft Office Outlook 2007. You can use the Journal folder to keep track of documents, phone calls, meetings, and other items and events that occur during the day. Outlook can even record many items in the Journal automatically. For example, you can configure Outlook to keep track of the amount of time you spend working in documents in Word, Excel, and other Office applications.

This section explains how to use the Journal to add items manually and how to configure the Journal to track items automatically.

Add and View Journal Items

Outlook allows you to record Journal entries for contacts from within the Contacts folder. For example, you can create a Journal entry about a telephone conversation you had with a customer. The entry can include the name of the person you spoke with, the time it took place, the length of the call, the topic of conversation, and other information. You can also record other events and tasks in the Journal.

Add a Journal Item in the Journal Folder

① Click the Journal icon on the Navigation Pane to open the Journal folder.

② Click No when prompted to automatically journal Microsoft Office documents.

③ Click New in the toolbar to open a new Journal item.

④ Type a subject for the Journal item.

⑤ Choose an Entry Type from the drop-down list.

⑥ If you are recording a timed event, click the Start Time button to start tracking time.

⑦ Click Pause Timer when you finish the activity.

⑧ Click Categorize and choose a color category if desired.

(continued on the next page)

Tip

If the Journal icon does not appear in the Navigation Pane, click Configure Buttons at the bottom right corner of the Navigation Pane, choose Add Or Remove Buttons, and choose the Journal folder.

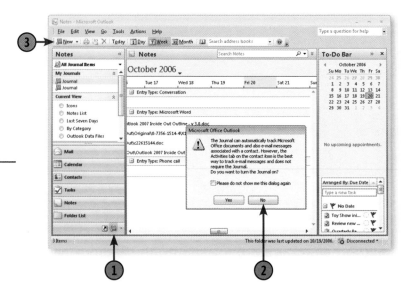

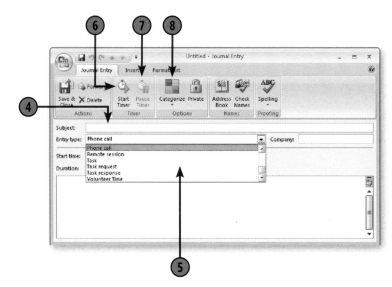

Add a Journal Item in the Journal Folder *(continued)*

9 Click Address Book and associate a contact with the Journal item.

10 Use the Insert and Format Text tabs on the ribbon to access other features.

11 Click Save & Close.

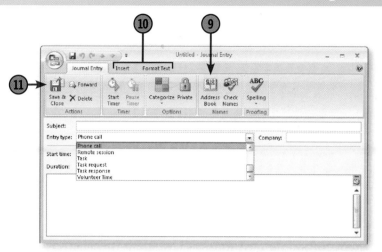

Tip

You can click Activities in the Show group of a contact form's ribbon to view activities associated with that contact. These activities include e-mail messages, appointments, and other Office Outlook items that are associated with that contact. The resulting Activities pane provides a list of these items, making it easy to find, for example, messages you have sent or received from the contact.

Try This!

When you have a Journal entry open, you can start or stop a timer that keeps track of the time you spend working on that entry. For instance, if you open a Journal entry associated with a certain document, you can click Start Timer, open the associated document, work on that document, close it, and then choose Pause Timer. Journal records the duration you spend working on that document. This can, for example, allow you to track the billable hours you spend on a project.

Log a Telephone Call

(1) Click the Contacts icon on the Navigation Pane.

(2) Click a contact.

(3) Choose Create from the Actions menu.

(4) Choose New Journal Entry For Contact from the submenu.

(5) Make any necessary changes in the Journal Entry window, such as editing the subject, adding notes, or specifying length of time.

(6) Click Save & Close.

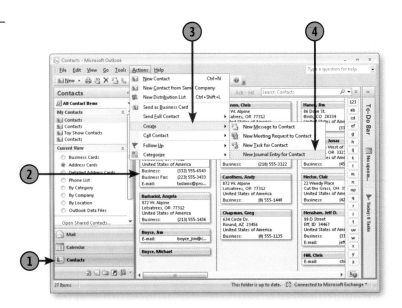

See Also

For information on viewing phone call entries in a list, see "View Journal Items as a List" on page 198.

Tip

If you forget to click the Start Timer or Pause Timer buttons when placing the call, you can simply type the duration of the call in the Duration field, setting it to whatever amount of time you spent on the call

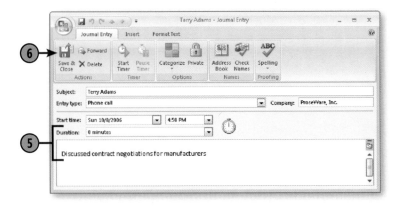

View Journal Items in a Timeline

1. Click the Journal icon in the Navigation Pane to open the Journal folder.

2. View items in the timeline.

3. Use the scrollbar to move through the timeline.

4. Click and type text to search the Journal for specific items.

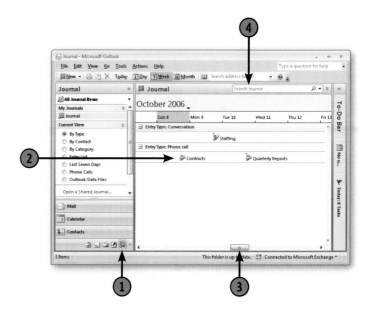

Tip

As in other folders, you can view the Journal folder using one of several predefined views. You can also create your own custom views of the Journal. The default view is Timeline, which shows items in relation to the time they were recorded.

View Journal Items as a List

1 Click the Journal icon in the Navigation Pane to open the Journal folder.

2 Click Entry List in the Navigation Pane.

3 Double-click the associated file to open it in the application in which it was created.

4 Click column headers to sort the Journal items by the selected column.

5 Choose other views from the Navigation Pane.

A list view lets you see a more complete list of Journal items without having to search through the timeline.

See Also

For information on using Journal entries to describe a tele-phone call, see "Recording Journal Entries" on page 132.

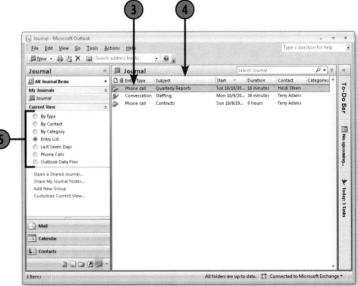

Create Journal Items Automatically

The Outlook Journal can keep track of when you worked on something in Outlook or in a supported application, such as Microsoft Word or Microsoft Access. You can configure the Journal to record activities you perform on an item, such as creating an e-mail message or updating a specific contact.

Track Time Spent on Documents and Other Items

① In Outlook, choose Options from the Tools menu.

② Click Journal Options on the Preferences tab.

③ Choose the types of events you want Outlook to record automatically.

④ Choose the contacts for whom you want these events recorded.

⑤ Choose the types of files for which you want Outlook to track time.

⑥ Specify what you want Outlook to do when you double-click a Journal item.

⑦ Click OK.

⑧ Click OK.

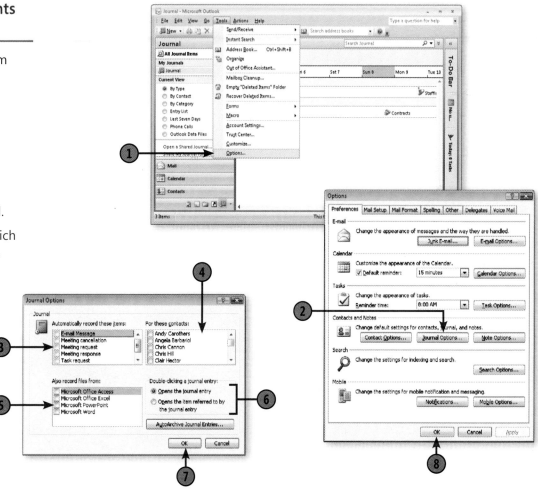

Turn Off Automatic Journaling

1. In Outlook, choose Options from the Tools menu.

2. Click Journal Options on the Preferences tab.

3. Deselect all of the check boxes for event types.

4. Deselect all of the check boxes for file types.

5. Deselect all of the contacts.

6. Specify what you want Outlook to do when you double-click a Journal item.

7. Click OK.

8. Click OK.

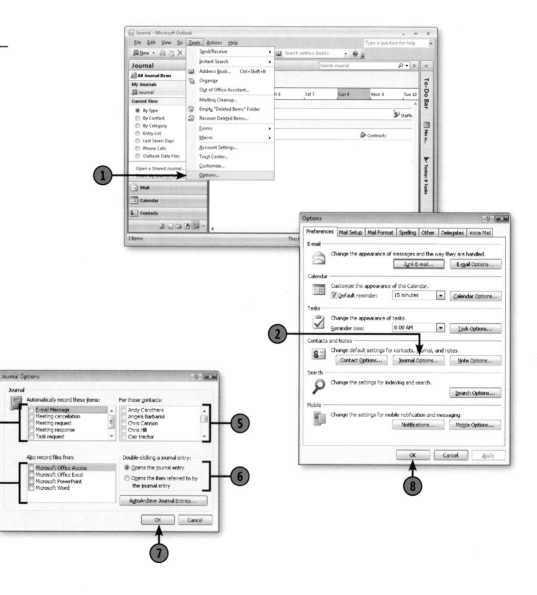

Managing Items and Folders

Microsoft Office Outlook 2007 provides several ways you can manage your Outlook items and folders, including organizing items in categories, creating and using folders to store items, using the Mailbox Cleanup tool, and using the Journal to organize your work. For example, you can create folders to store e-mail messages relating to projects on which you work, making it easier to locate those messages when you need them.

Categories let you organize and sort your data in Outlook. You might assign a project category to all items for a specific project and then set up a view in each Outlook folder that displays the items grouped by category. This helps you quickly locate items associated with a specific project. Outlook 2007 adds color to categories, making them even more useful—you can now tell at a glance the categories assigned to specific items.

This section covers how to manage your items and folders in Outlook 2007. It covers how to categorize items, organize folders, delete items, and clean up folders.

Using Categories

Categories are colors with associated keywords or phrases that help you manage Outlook items, such as contacts, e-mail messages, journal entries, and meetings. With categories, you can set up relationships between items stored in different places in Outlook. For example, you can categorize a piece of e-mail and a meeting reminder as business items. Then when you sort, filter, or search for all your business-related items, that e-mail message and meeting reminder appear. The addition of color to categories in Outlook 2007 lets you tell at a glance what categories are assigned to an item.

Categorize an Item

1. Select an item.
2. Click Categorize on the Standard toolbar.
3. Choose a category to assign to the item.
4. A category indicator appears in the Categories column and in the header.

Tip

You can associate an item with as many categories as you like. The more categories with which you associate an item, the easier it is to find when you conduct searches.

Tip

You can also choose Categorize from the Edit menu, and then choose a category from the resulting cascading menu.

If this is the first time you have used the category, Outlook asks if you want to change the color. For now, just click No. You learn about changing category properties later in this section.

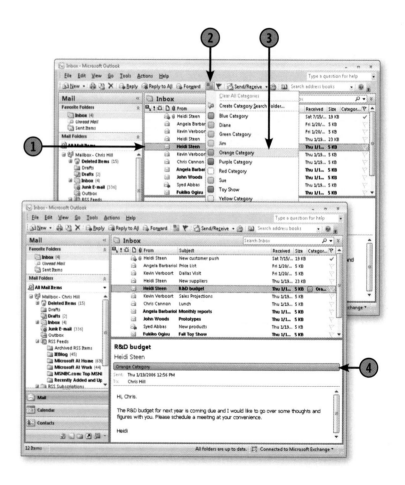

Assign Multiple Categories

① Select an item.

② Click Categorize on the Standard toolbar.

③ Choose All Categories.

④ Place a check beside each category you want to assign.

⑤ Click OK.

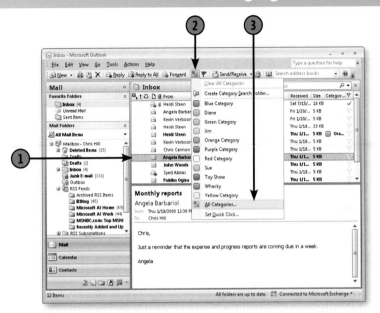

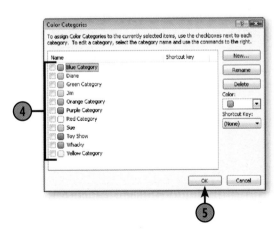

Add Categories to Your Category List

1. Select an item.

2. Click Categorize on the Standard toolbar.

3. Choose All Categories.

4. Click New.

5. In the Add New Category dialog box that appears, type a new category name in the Name field.

6. Select a color.

7. Choose a shortcut key (if desired).

8. Click OK.

9. The new category appears in the Color Categories dialog box.

10. Deselect the check box if you only want to create the category but not assign it yet.

11. Click OK.

Caution

If you assign a category to an item and then remove it from the Master Category list, the category is not deleted from that item. You can still sort, view, or filter items based on deleted categories.

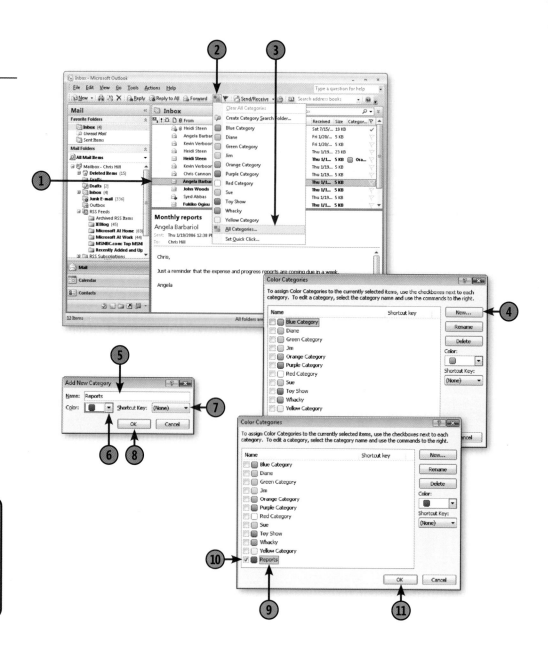

Rename a Category

① Select an item.

② Click Categorize on the Standard toolbar.

③ Choose All Categories.

④ Click the category.

⑤ Click Rename.

⑥ Type a new name and press Enter.

⑦ Click OK

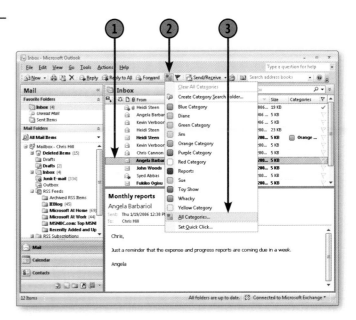

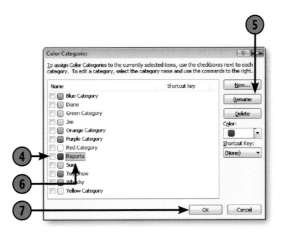

Delete a Category

① Select an item.

② Click Categorize on the Standard toolbar.

③ Choose All Categories.

④ Click the category you want to delete.

⑤ Click Delete.

Tip

Deleting a category that is in use only clears the color from the category. To remove the category altogether, you must clear the category from all items where it is used.

Tip

If you want to clear a category from all items where it is used, arrange the view by category. Locate the grouped category you want to remove, select all of the items in the group, right-click an item in the group, click Categorize, and click the category you want to remove.

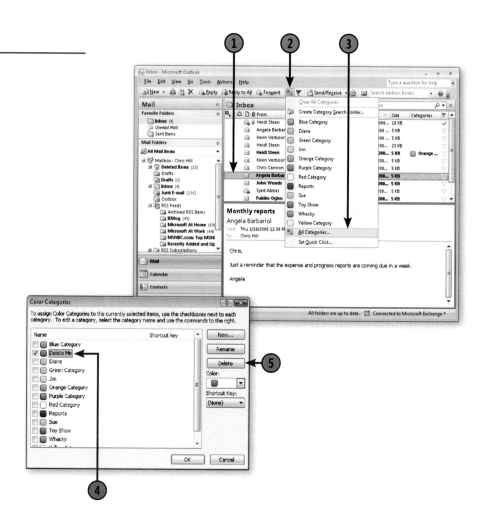

Using Search Folders

Search folders are a great feature that was added in Outlook 2003, and they have been made even better in Outlook 2007. Search folders enable you to quickly locate messages anywhere they exist in your Outlook data store. Although a search folder looks and behaves like any other Outlook folder, the search folder is really a special way to display search results. When you create the search folder, you specify the search conditions. Outlook then displays the results of the search in a folder-like way. However, the items that appear in the search folder actually reside in other locations—the search folder is just a way to group those messages together in one viewing location, regardless of where the messages are actually located.

Use an Existing Search Folder

1. Click the Mail icon.

2. Click to expand the Search Folders branch.

3. Click Unread Mail.

4. All unread messages appear in the message pane.

5. Click Categorized Mail.

6. All messages that have category assignments appear in the message pane.

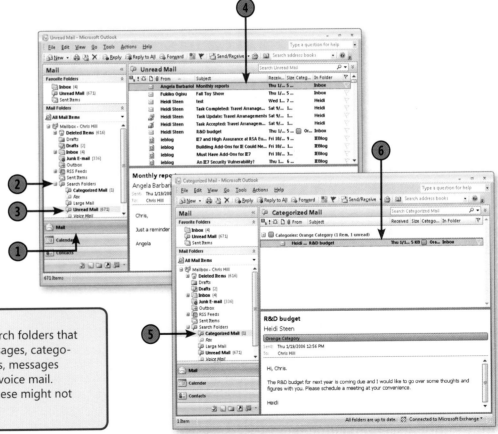

Tip

Outlook includes a handful of predefined search folders that you can use right away to locate unread messages, categorized messages, messages with attached faxes, messages larger than 100Kb, and messages containing voice mail. Depending on your configuration, some of these might not be available to you.

Create a Custom Search Folder

1. Click the Mail icon in the Navigation Pane.

2. Right-click Search Folders and choose New Search Folder.

3. Scroll to the bottom of the list.

4. Choose Create A Custom Search Folder.

5. Click Choose.

6. Type a name for the search folder.

7. Click Criteria.

(continued on the next page)

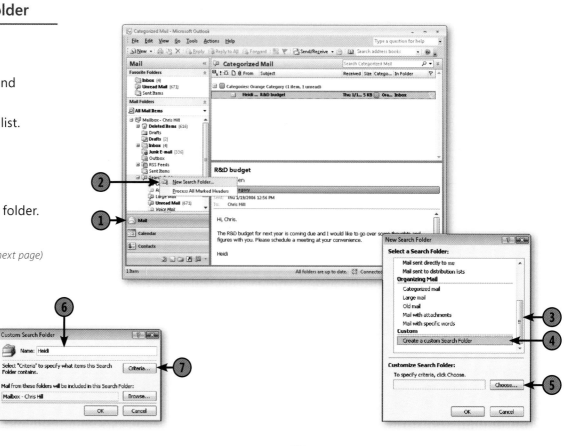

Tip

The Unread Mail search folder shows all unread messages, including those in folders other than the Inbox. Likewise, the Categorized Mail search folder shows all messages that have a category assigned from all folders in your mailbox. The Categorized Mail search folder does not show messages without a category assignment.

Tip

The options in the Search Folder Criteria dialog box give you a wide array of conditions to use in defining the search. For example, on the Messages tab you can search for words or phrases, specify that the message is from a particular sender or sent to a particular recipient, and set a time frame in which the message was sent or received (as well as other time options).

Create a Custom
Search Folder *(continued)*

⑧ Click From and choose a contact, or type an e-mail address in the text box.

⑨ Click OK.

⑩ Click OK.

⑪ Click OK.

⑫ Messages that fit the search condition appear in the message pane.

⑬ Click Inbox to view all messages in the Inbox.

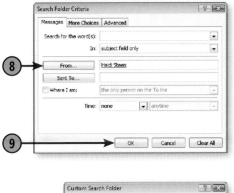

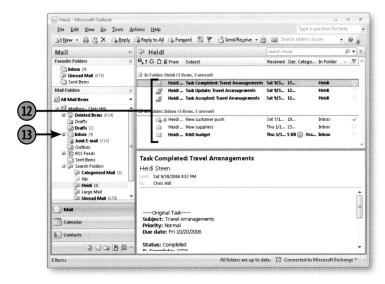

Modify a Search Folder

① Click the Mail icon on the Navigation Pane.

② Expand the Search Folders branch, if needed.

③ Right-click the search folder you want to modify.

④ Choose Customize This Search Folder.

⑤ Change the name, if desired.

⑥ Click Criteria.

⑦ Click the More Choices tab.

⑧ Place a check mark beside Only Items With.

⑨ Choose One Or More Attachments.

⑩ Click OK.

⑪ Click OK.

⑫ The results of the new search criteria appear in the message pane.

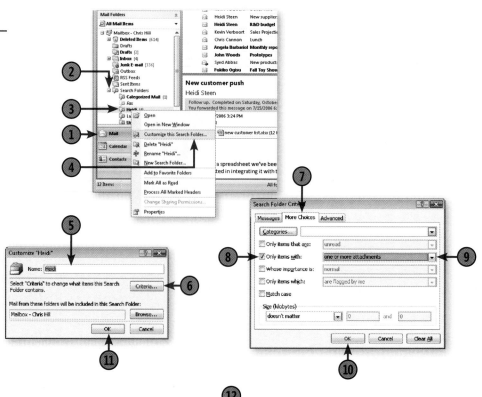

Tip

You can combine options on the More Choices tab to refine a search, such as searching for all messages with a specific category that have attachments and that are larger than a specified size (in Kb). The choices on the Messages and Other Choices tabs are naturally limited because of space. The Advanced tab lets you choose any of the message fields to include in the search criteria.

Organizing with Folders

Outlook 2007 uses folders to let you store items, such as e-mail messages and notes. Outlook folders are similar to the folders you can create and modify in Windows Explorer in that they help organize items. The Inbox folder, for example, is the default location for your incoming e-mail messages. The Outbox folder, on the other hand, stores your outgoing e-mail messages until you send them.

You can use the existing folders created automatically by Outlook, but you can also create your own folders to help you organize your items in a way that makes the most sense for the way you use Outlook.

Create a New Folder

① In Outlook, choose New from the File menu and then Folder from the submenu.

② In the Create New Folder dialog box that appears, type a new folder name in the Name text box.

③ Select the type of item that the folder will contain from the Folder Contains drop-down list. For example, if you want a folder to store messages, select Mail And Post Items.

④ Select the location where you want the new folder to be placed.

⑤ Click OK.

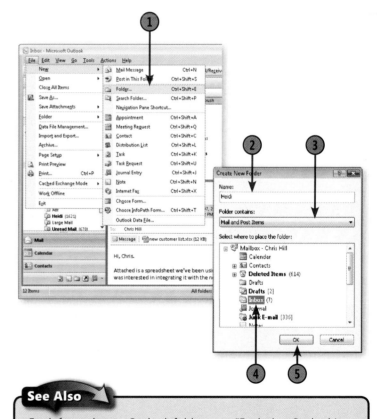

Tip

You can create subfolders, which are folders within folders. Subfolders can help you manage your items in Outlook by letting you organize items in ways that help you do your work. For example, you can set up subfolders under a new folder you created for messages relating to various aspects of a project on which you currently are working. As you receive e-mail relating to those aspects, you can move the item from the Inbox to the appropriate subfolder.

See Also

For information on Outlook folders, see "Exploring Outlook's Folders" on page 32.

Move Items to a Folder

1 In the Outlook main window, choose the item you want to move.

2 Click and drag the item from the message pane to the folder where you want to move the message.

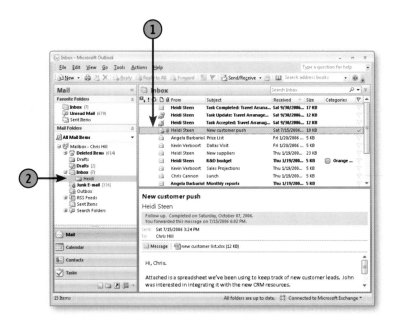

Move Items Without Dragging

1. Right-click the message you want to move, and choose Move To Folder.

2. In the Move Items dialog box that appears, click the target folder.

3. Click OK.

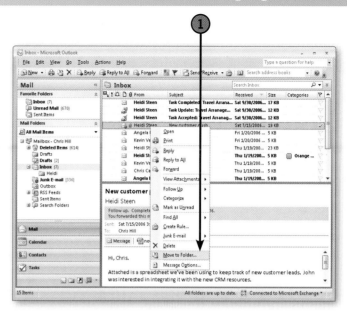

Try This!

When you move or copy an item, drag it while right-clicking instead of left-clicking. When you drop the item on a new folder, a shortcut menu appears. Choose Move, Copy, or Cancel to complete the operation.

Caution

Sometimes when you move an item you may drop it into the wrong folder. If you do this, don't panic. Choose Undo Move from the Edit menu immediately after you move the item. Outlook returns the item to its original location.

See Also

To learn how to move messages to other folders automatically with rules see "Working with the Rules Wizard" on page 88.

Cleaning Up Folders

You should get in the habit of cleaning out unwanted e-mail messages, old contacts, and other items by deleting them or moving them to other folders. Outlook 2007 provides the Mailbox Cleanup tool to help you manage your mailbox.

This tool lets you reduce the size of your mailbox to increase Outlook's performance and to make managing mailbox items easier.

Use the Mailbox Cleanup Tool

① In Outlook, choose Mailbox Cleanup from the Tools menu.

② In the Mailbox Cleanup dialog box that appears, click View Mailbox Size to display the Folder Size dialog box.

(continued on the next page)

See Also

For information on setting Auto-Archive options, see "Set the AutoArchive Options" on page 230

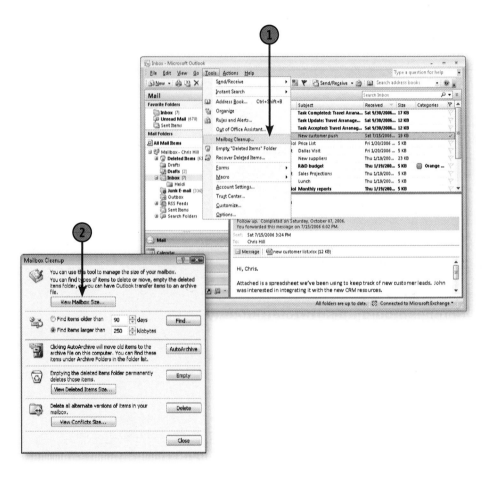

Use the Mailbox Cleanup Tool *(continued)*

③ View the size of your mailbox and other Outlook folders.

④ Click Close to close the Folder Size dialog box and return to the Mailbox Cleanup dialog box.

⑤ Click AutoArchive to immediately begin archiving items based on the settings you have defined for AutoArchive. The Mailbox Cleanup dialog box will close automatically while your mail is archived.

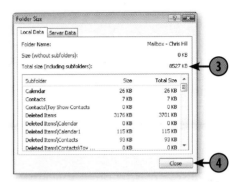

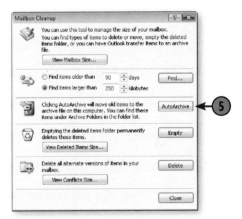

Caution !

Depending on the AutoArchive options set for a folder, messages older than a specific date may be removed from your current folders and placed in the Archive Folders. If you want to access a message that has been moved to these folders, open the folders from the Folder List pane and view the message in the main Outlook window.

Tip ✓

You can use the two search options on the Mailbox Cleanup dialog box to search for messages that are older than a specified length of time or that are larger than a specified size. In the resulting search results window you can select items and delete them from your mailbox. To delete these items, first select them in the results pane, then right-click the items and choose Delete, or simply select the items and press the Del key on the keyboard.

Tip ✓

Click View Deleted Items Size to view the amount of space taken up by your Deleted Items folder. Click Empty to permanently delete all items in the Deleted Items folder.

Deleting Items

Over time, your Outlook folders may become cluttered with too many items and become unmanageable. Outlook allows you to delete items from their current folder when you no longer need them. When you delete an item, it is removed from its current folder and placed in the Deleted Items folder.

Deleting an Item

1. In an Outlook folder, choose the item you want to delete.

2. Click Delete on the toolbar.

Caution

When you delete an item from within Outlook, no prompt appears asking if you are sure you want to delete the item. Outlook immediately moves it to the Deleted Items folder. If you delete an item by mistake, choose Undo from the Edit menu before continuing with any other tasks. You can also open the Deleted Items folder and drag the deleted item back to its original location.

Emptying the Deleted Items Folder

① In the Navigation Pane, right-click the Deleted Items folder.

② Choose Empty "Deleted Items" Folder.

③ Click Yes to empty the Deleted Items folder.

Try This!

To set up Outlook to empty the Deleted Items folder when you exit Outlook, choose Options from the Tools menu. Click the Other tab, then select Empty The Deleted Items Folder Upon Exiting. Click OK.

See Also

For information on managing the Inbox Folder, including deleting unneeded messages, see "Managing the Inbox Folder" on page 78.

Caution

If you configure Outlook to empty the Deleted Items folder on exit, keep in mind that all items in the Deleted Items folder are permanently deleted when you exit Outlook. They will no longer be available in the Deleted Items Folder the next time you start Outlook.

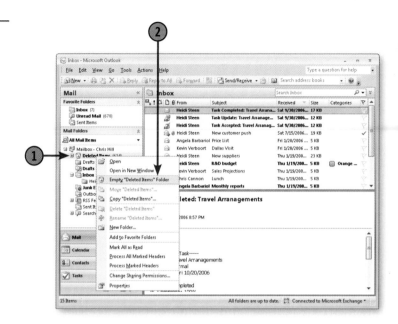

Managing Your Outlook Files

Outlook stores your data in special types of files called *Outlook data files*. The main type of file is a personal folder file, or PST file. Outlook can store a complete set of Outlook folders—in addition to custom folders you add—in a PST file. For example, a particular PST would include Calendar, Inbox, and Tasks folders, along with custom folders.

In addition to storing data in PST files, Outlook can store data in a Microsoft Exchange Server mailbox. The mailbox resides on the server rather than on your computer. When you open Outlook, the program contacts the server to display your data.

Sometimes your computer cannot communicate with the server because the server is offline or because you may be working on a computer that isn't connected to the network. In these situations, Outlook can use a set of offline folders stored in an offline folder file, or OST file. Outlook stores data in the OST file and synchronizes the changes with the mailbox the next time it is able to connect to the server.

This section explains how to perform several tasks with your Outlook data files, including adding new data files, using an existing file, and importing and exporting items. The section also explains how to back up and restore your Outlook data in a PST file and how to archive items

Working with Outlook Data Files

Unless your only e-mail account is on an Exchange Server, Outlook creates a local data file for you when you set up your Outlook profile. When Exchange Server is the only account, Outlook stores all items in your Exchange Server mailbox. You can easily create a new PST file and then add or remove folders to it as needed.

Tip

When you add an Exchange Server account to an Outlook 2007 profile, Outlook automatically sets up the account for Cached Exchange Mode, which makes a local copy of your mailbox. Items are still stored on the server, even though Outlook also keeps a cached local copy.

Create a New Data File

1. In Outlook, choose Data File Management from the File menu to open the Account Settings dialog box.

2. View the existing data files, if any, on the Data Files tab.

3. Click Add to open the New Outlook Data File dialog box.

4. With Office Outlook Personal Folders File (.pst) selected, click OK to open the Create Or Open Outlook Data File dialog box.

(continued on the next page)

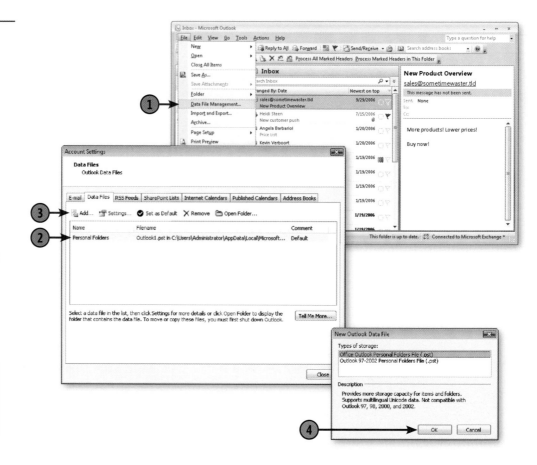

See Also

For more information on working with Outlook folders, see "Exploring Outlook's Folders" on page 32.

Create a New Data File *(continued)*

(5) If you need to choose a different location, click Browse Folders to expand the dialog box so you can choose a different folder.

(6) Type a name for the PST file.

(7) Click OK to open the Create Microsoft Personal Folders dialog box.

(8) Change the name (if desired) to differentiate this set of folders from your others.

(9) Specify a password for the file (optional).

(10) Select this option if you want Outlook to store the password in your Windows password list so you don't have to type the password each time you use the file.

(11) Click OK to return to the Outlook Data Files dialog box

(12) Click Close.

(13) The new set of folders appears in your folder list.

Try This!

You can easily add folders to your new set of personal folders. Open Outlook, right-click in the folder list, and choose New Folder. Select a location in the new folder set, specify a name for the new folder, select the folder type, and click OK to create the new folder.

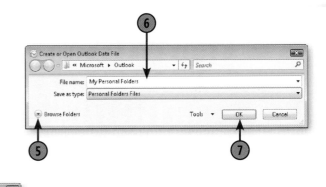

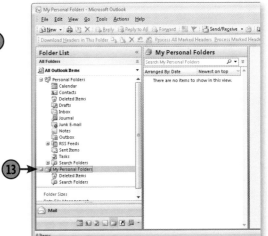

You can select an existing PST file in the Create Or Open Outlook Data File dialog box rather than create a new one. This is a good method for moving a PST file from one computer to another. To accomplish that feat, copy the PST to the new computer, open Outlook, and add the existing PST to your profile. You will then be able to access all of the items in the old PST.

Importing and Exporting Items

Although you probably do much of your work in Outlook, occasionally you might want to move data into Outlook from other programs or export data from Outlook to another program. Outlook makes it easy to import and export items. This section focuses on how to import and export items to and from PST files.

See Also

For more information on importing other types of data, see "Importing Data From Another Program" on page 40.

Import Items into Outlook

1. Choose Import And Export from the File menu to open the Import And Export Wizard.

2. Select Import From Another Program Or File.

3. Click Next.

4. Select Personal Folder File.

5. Click Next.

(continued on the next page)

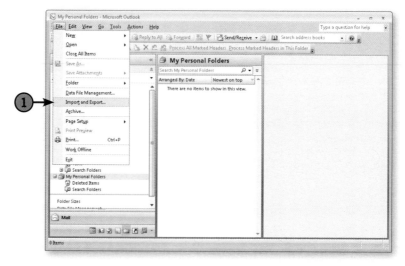

Tip

You can use the import feature in Outlook to import messages and other items from other PST files, contacts from an Access database or Excel spreadsheet to your Contacts folder, and other types of information.

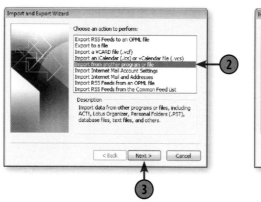

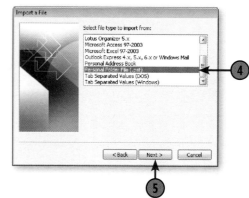

Import Items into Outlook *(continued)*

(6) Click Browse to locate the PST file from which you want to import.

(7) Select an option to specify how you want duplicate items to be handled.

(8) Click Next.

(9) Select the folder from which you want to import items.

(10) Click Filter to open the Filter dialog box.

(11) Specify options that define (filter) the data that Outlook will import.

(12) Click OK

(13) Click Finish.

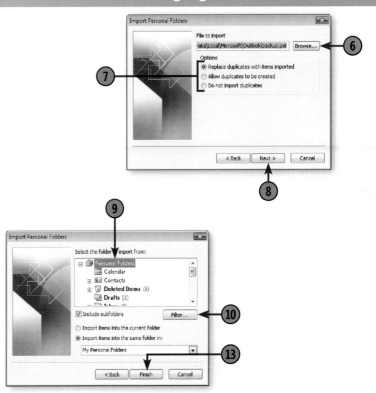

Tip

Importing selected items from a PST file gives you an easy way to selectively copy Outlook items from one computer to another. Simply copy the PST file from the source computer to the destination computer, and then use the Import feature to import only those items you want on the other computer.

Tip

You can use the Filter dialog box to selectively import items. For example, perhaps you only want to import items that have the category Personal assigned to them. Or maybe you only want to import messages that came from specific senders. Whatever the case, the Filter dialog box lets you control which items are imported.

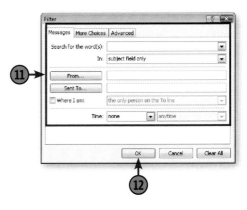

Export Items from Outlook

1 Choose Import And Export from the File menu to open the Import And Export Wizard.

2 Select Export To A File

3 Click Next.

4 Select Personal Folder File(.pst).

5 Click Next.

(continued on the next page)

Tip

You don't have to export to a new PST file. You can export items to an existing PST file. This gives you a handy means of selectively backing up or archiving specific items. For example, you might back up selected items from your Exchange Server mailbox to a PST file on your local computer for safekeeping.

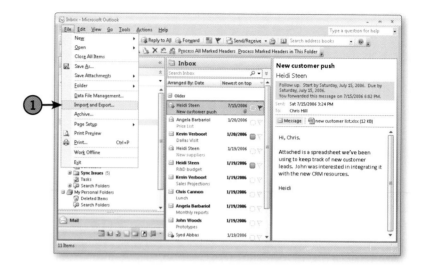

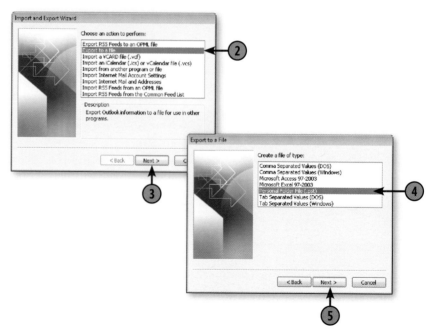

Export Items from Outlook *(continued)*

(6) Select the folder from which you want to export items.

(7) Click Filter to open the Filter dialog box.

(8) Specify options that control (filter) the data that Outlook will import, such as in this example of items created last month.

(9) Click OK

(10) Click Next.

(11) Specify the path and name of the file to which you want to export, or click Browse to select a file.

(12) Specify how you want duplicate items to be handled.

(13) Click Finish.

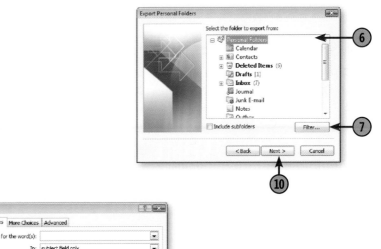

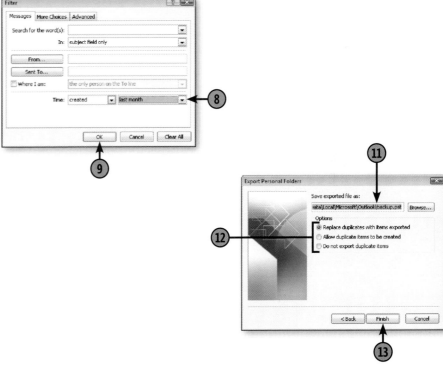

See Also

For more information on creating and using Outlook files, see "Working With Outlook Data Files" on page 220.

Tip

If you specify a file in Step 11 that does not exist, Outlook will display the Create Microsoft Personal Folders dialog box after you click Finish. Simply click OK to create the file and complete the export process.

Backing Up and Restoring a Data File

If you use a set of personal folders in a PST file as your only data store or in addition to an Exchange Server mailbox, back up that PST file so your data is still available if your computer experiences a problem such as a failed hard drive. Having the PST file backed up allows you to restore the file and recover your data. You can back up smaller files to a floppy disk, but larger files must be backed up to your hard drive, a removable disk, or other media.

Back Up Outlook Data

① Choose Data File Management from the File menu to open the Account Settings dialog box.

(continued on the next page)

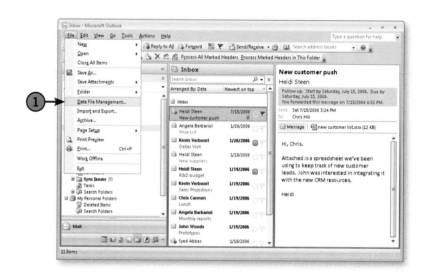

Caution

Don't back up your PST file to the same hard drive where it is currently located. If the drive fails, you will lose both copies of the file. Instead, back up the file to another hard drive if your computer has more than one or to another backup disk, CD, or tape.

Tip

Set up a regular backup schedule for your PST file, and make sure you back it up frequently to avoid losing any data.

Back Up Outlook Data *(continued)*

② Double-click the folder you want to back up to open the Personal Folders dialog box for the file.

③ Click in the Filename field, and use the arrow keys on the keyboard to view the whole path for the file. Make note of the file name and location.

④ Click OK.

⑤ Click Close, and then close Outlook. You can now locate the file on your hard drive and manually create and store a backup copy in a safe location.

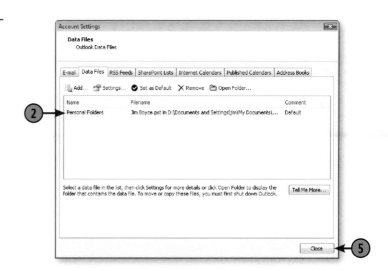

Caution

Make sure you close Outlook before making a backup copy of your PST file.

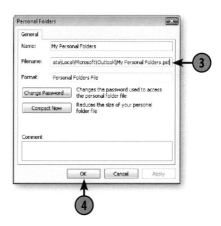

Tip

You can use a backup program to back up the PST file if you don't want to copy it manually, or if you need to copy it to tape or CD-R/CD-RW. All versions of Windows include a Backup program in the Accessories menu that you can use to back up the file. CD-R and CD-RW drives usually include software you can use to copy files to a CD. The advantage to using a backup program to back up your PST file is that the backup program keeps track of the file's original location and restores the file to that location by default. This saves you the trouble of trying to remember the file's original location.

Restore Outlook Data

① Close Outlook, and then use Computer (My Computer in Windows XP and earlier) to open the folder containing the backup file.

② Click on the file you want to restore.

③ Right-click the file and choose Copy.

(continued on the next page)

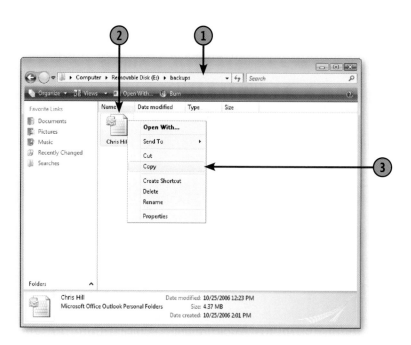

Restore Outlook Data *(continued)*

④ Open the original location for the file. This location is the one recorded in the Personal Folders dialog box for the file, as described in the previous procedure.

⑤ Right-click and choose Paste.

⑥ Open Outlook, and verify that your data items are intact.

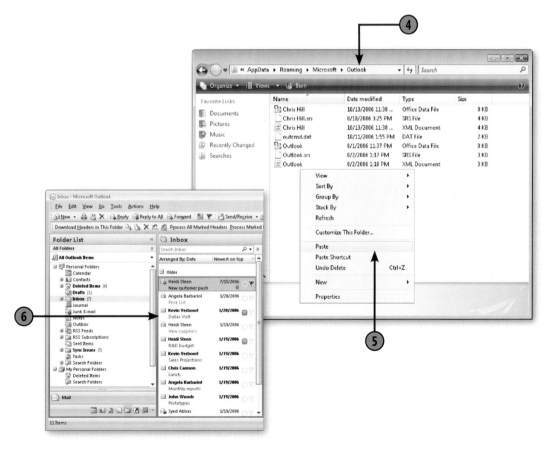

Archiving Outlook Data Files

Old messages, tasks, and other items have a tendency to pile up unless you clean them out. Outlook provides an AutoArchive feature that lets you specify how often Outlook should clean out old items, where it should place those items (or whether it should delete them), which items to move, and so on. If you choose to archive items rather than delete them, Outlook places them in a PST file of your choosing. You can then recover them by opening that set of folders and copying the items back to your regular folders or by using the Import feature in Outlook to import from the archive file.

Set the AutoArchive Options

1 Choose Options from the Tools menu to display the Options dialog box.

2 Click the Other tab.

3 Click AutoArchive to open the AutoArchive dialog box.

(continued on the next page)

Tip

A network administrator can set retention policies that control your AutoArchive settings, preventing certain archive operations you might otherwise configure through your AutoArchive settings.

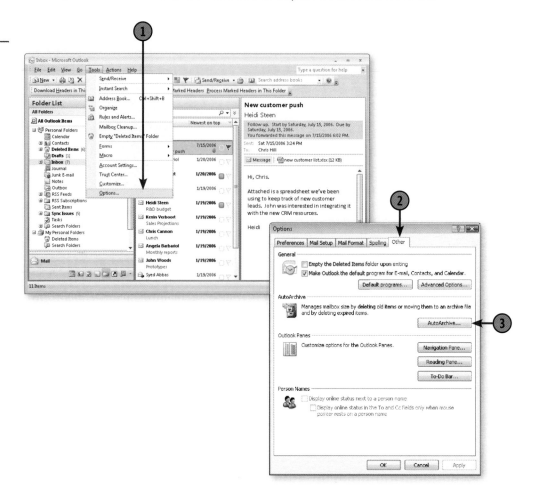

Set the AutoArchive Options *(continued)*

4 Select the options that will control the AutoArchive function, including its frequency, how old messages should be before they are archived, and whether items should be moved to another folder.

5 Click to set archive options for all folders according to the settings in the dialog box.

6 Click OK.

7 Click OK to close the Options dialog box.

Caution !

Select the Prompt Before AutoArchive Runs option if you want to be able to control whether Outlook archives items. If this option is not selected, Outlook performs the archive operation without warning you.

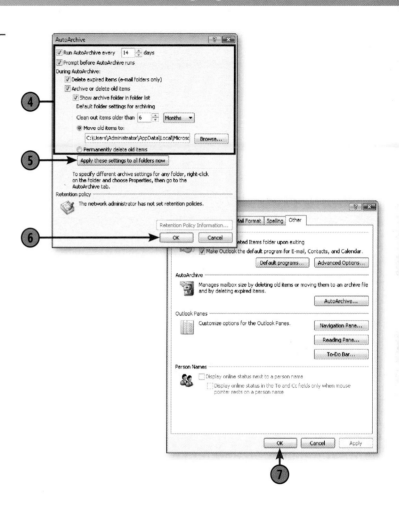

Archive an Outlook Data File

① Choose Archive from the File menu to open the Archive dialog box.

② Select this option if you want to archive all folders using the AutoArchive settings.

③ Select this option if you want to archive only the selected folder and its subfolders.

④ Select the folder from which you want to archive items.

⑤ Specify how old items must be to be archived.

⑥ Select this option to archive items that would otherwise be skipped because you have configured them not to AutoArchive.

⑦ Select the file where you want to store the archived items.

⑧ Click OK to archive the items.

⑨ Close the dialog box.

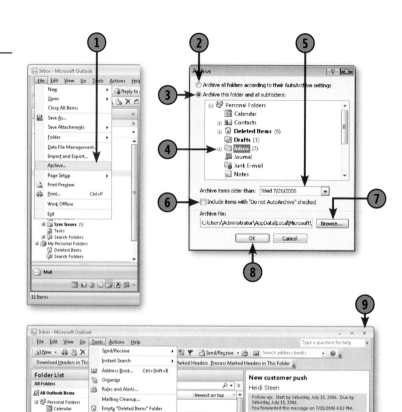

See Also

For more information on backing up PST files, see "Backing Up and Restoring a Data File" on page 226.

Tip

Back up your archive file each time you back up your PST file to make sure you can recover archived items if a system or drive failure causes you to lose your regular archive file.

Try This!

Test your ability to recover archived items. Open the AutoArchive dialog box, and note the location of your archive file. Review the "Import Items into Outlook" task earlier in this chapter and import a selection of items from your archive PST file.

Working with Offline Folders

When you use an Exchange Server mailbox, Outlook stores your data in the mailbox. As long as the server is available, you can access your data. If the server is offline or you're not connected to the network, you can't continue working with your mailbox data unless you configure a set of offline folders and set Outlook to use Cached Exchange Mode. In this mode, Outlook uses the offline folders as a temporary storage location for your data until you can connect to the server once again. Then Outlook synchronizes any changes between the mailbox and the offline folders.

By default, Outlook configures an Exchange Server account to use Cached Exchange Mode. However, if you turn it off or an administrator preconfigures a profile for you without Cached Exchange Mode, you can enable it on an existing account.

Configure Outlook for Cached Exchange Mode

1. Choose Account Settings from the Tools menu.
2. In the Account Settings dialog box that appears, click the Exchange Server account on the E-mail tab.
3. Click Change.
4. Select the Use Cached Exchange Mode option.
5. Click Next.
6. Click Finish.
7. Close and restart Outlook.

Tip

Your computer must be connected to the Exchange Server the first time you start Outlook with Cached Exchange Mode to enable Outlook to retrieve a locally cached copy of your mailbox.

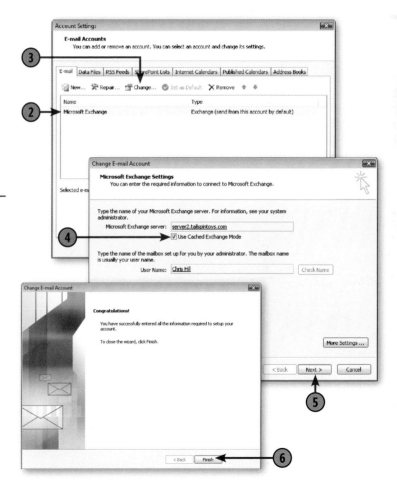

Synchronize Offline Folders

① Click Send/Receive on the Standard toolbar.

② View the progress of the synchronization in the Outlook Send/Receive Progress dialog box.

> **See Also**
>
> For more information on sending and receiving e-mail, see "Receiving E-Mail" on page 74.

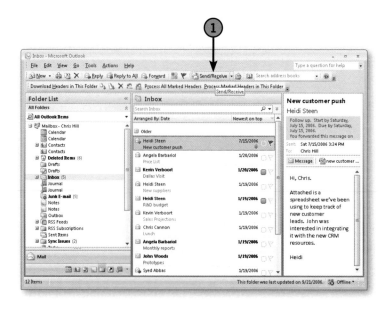

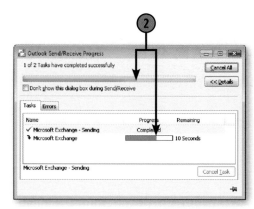

14

Customizing Outlook

Although Microsoft Office Outlook 2007 can be used out of the box, one of its finest features is its ability to be customized to look and work the way you work. You can customize Microsoft Outlook in a number of ways. You can choose formats for messages to customize outgoing mail messages. With Calendar, you can set up holiday schedules to match those recognized by your business or organization, and specify your workweek. For example, if your workweek differs from the traditional 8:00 a.m. to 5:00 p.m., Monday through Friday, you can change Outlook's Calendar views to match the days and hours you work.

You also can specify how Contact items are sorted. Finally, you can customize Outlook's toolbars and the Navigation Pane.

Using Read and Delivery Receipts

Outlook can help you manage your e-mail messages by keeping track of when messages that you send are delivered and read by their recipients. This is handy when you send a time-sensitive e-mail and you want to know when the recipients received and read the message.

Use Read and Delivery Receipts on Individual Messages

1. Open the Inbox and click New to start a new e-mail message.

2. Click the Options tab on the ribbon.

3. Select the Request A Delivery Receipt option.

4. Select the Request A Read Receipt option.

5. Click Send to send the message as you normally would. Outlook sends you a delivery receipt when the message is delivered.

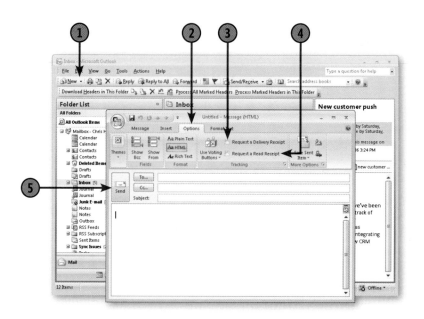

Tip

In the Message Options dialog box, you can set priority levels for an e-mail message. Click the Importance drop-down list, and select Low, Normal, or High. Low or High importance messages are sent at the same speed as Normal, but the recipient will see a symbol indicating the message's importance.

Try This!

To set Outlook so all messages have a delivery and read receipt, choose Options from the Tools menu and click E-Mail Options on the Preferences tab. Click Tracking Options, and select Read Receipt and Delivery Receipt.

Choosing Message Formats

When you create new e-mail messages, you can specify the format in which the message should be created. The format you choose must be supported by the recipient of the message. Outlook also allows you to set up your environment so that all your messages use the same format. You can choose from Plain Text, Rich Text, or HTML as the default.

Select a Format for the Open Message

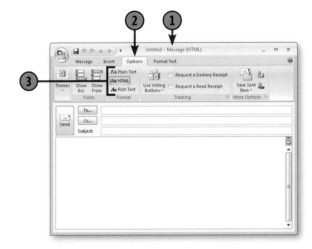

① Create a new message.

② Click the Options tab on the ribbon.

③ Choose a format from the Format group:

- Choose Plain Text to create a message without formatting.

- Choose HTML to create a message with HTML support, such as embedded tables, inserted pictures, and live hyperlinks.

- Choose Rich Text to create a message with rich text formatting support, such as embedded objects, font specifications, and colored text.

Tip

You can change the formatting of a message you have received by using the Format menu's Plain, Rich Text, and HTML commands.

See Also

For information on using Rich Text or HTML message formats, see "Formatting Message Text" on page 59.

Tip

If you are not sure of the format that your recipient can read, use the Plain Text option. This ensures nothing is lost in the translation if your recipient's e-mail program does not support Rich Text or HTML messages.

Select a Default Message Format

① Choose Options from the Tools menu.

② Click the Mail Format tab.

③ Click the Compose In This Message Format drop-down list and choose the format you want to use for all your messages.

④ Click OK.

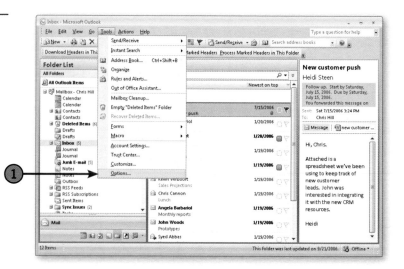

See Also

For more on formatting information in your messages, see "Add Formatting to a Message" on page 60.

Tip

When you use HTML formatting, your messages can include pictures that are located on the Internet. If you want to embed a picture instead of creating a hyperlink to it (which would require the recipients to have an Internet connection to view the picture), click Picture in the Illustrations group of the ribbon's Insert tab. In the Insert Picture dialog box, click in the file name field and type the URL to the picture, such as www.boyce.us/images/jim.jpg, and then click Insert. Outlook retrieves a copy of the image and embeds it in the message.

Try This!

If your default format is HTML but you know that a recipient's e-mail program does not support HTML-formatted messages, create a new message and choose Plain Text on the Options tab.

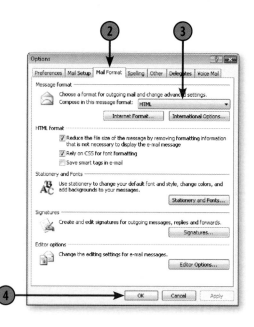

Setting Calendar Options

Outlook enables you to change the way Calendar works. You can change the default Monday–Friday work week to one that is specific to your schedule (perhaps you work Wednesday–Saturday). You also can set up holidays that are not traditionally observed in the United States.

Set the Work Week

① Choose Options from the Tools menu.

② Click Calendar Options on the Preferences tab.

③ Select the days of the week that you work.

④ Click the Start Time drop-down list, and select the time your workday begins.

⑤ Do the same in the End Time list for the end of your workday.

⑥ Click OK.

⑦ Click OK.

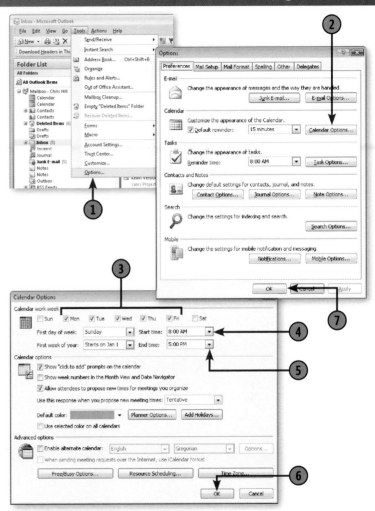

Try This!

Change your work hours to begin at 12:00 a.m. and end at 7:00 a.m. Click the Calendar icon on the Navigation Pane and click the Day View button on the Standard toolbar. Notice how the 12–7 range is shown in white to indicate your workday hours. Also, note that you cannot specify a start time from the previous day. For example, if your work "day" runs from 11:00 p.m. to 7:00 a.m. the next morning, you cannot specify those start and end times. Instead, you would have to specify 12:00 a.m. as your start time.

Tip

You can specify which day of the week is the first day for you. Click the First Day Of Week drop-down list, and click a day.

Setting Calendar Options **239**

Add Holidays

① Choose Options from the Tools menu.

② Click Calendar Options on the Preferences tab.

③ Click Add Holidays.

④ Select the country that includes the holidays you want to add to your Calendar.

⑤ Click OK.

⑥ Click OK.

⑦ Click OK.

Tip

If you want to add a nontraditional holiday to Calendar, set it up as an event in your Calendar folder.

See Also

For information on adding events to Calendar, see "Adding an Appointment" on page 138 and "Adding an Event" on page 141.

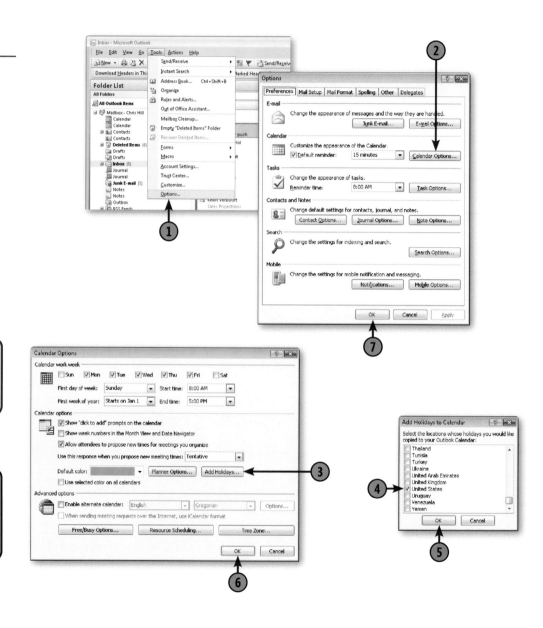

Customizing the Navigation Pane

The Navigation Pane includes icons you click to quickly open an Outlook folder. You can customize the Navigation Pane in several ways, such as by turning it off when you want more room to see items in Outlook or by adding a shortcut group to the icons displayed in the bar.

Show or Hide the Navigation Pane

1. Click the Minimize the Navigation Pane button.

2. The Navigation Pane minimizes.

3. Click the Expand the Navigation Pane button to expand the Navigation Pane again.

See Also

To learn more about the Navigation Pane, see "Exploring Outlook Folders" on page 32.

Tip

You also can hide the Navigation Pane by choosing Navigation Pane from the View menu and then choosing Minimized.

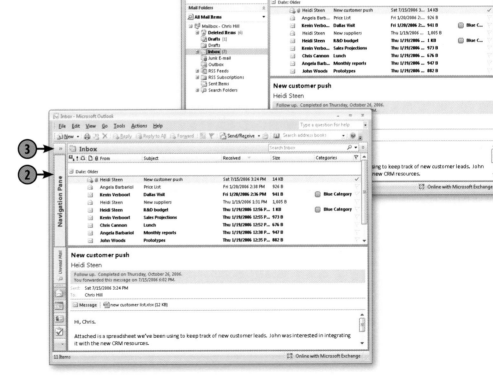

Add a Shortcut Group to the Navigation Pane

1 Click the Shortcuts button on the Navigation Pane.

2 Outlook displays the Shortcuts pane.

3 Click Add New Shortcut.

4 Choose the Outlook folder for which you want to create a shortcut.

5 Click OK.

(continued on the next page)

Try This!

Add several shortcut groups to help you access Outlook items you use often. For example, create a new contacts folder to store your personal contacts separately from your business contacts. Create a shortcut to that folder in the Shortcuts list. When you want to open that folder, just click its icon on the shortcut group. Add all of your most frequently used Outlook folders to the list.

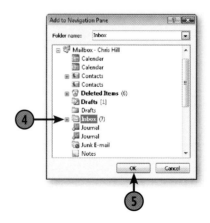

Add a Shortcut Group to the Navigation Pane *(continued)*

6 The folder shortcut appears in the Shortcuts list.

7 Click Add New Group.

8 Outlook adds a new group.

9 Type a new name for the group and press Enter.

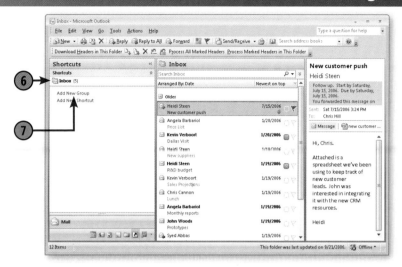

Tip

You can add shortcuts to your favorite Web sites on the Shortcuts list. Just create a shortcut on the Windows desktop to the Web site, and then drag the shortcut to the Shortcuts list in the Navigation Pane. You'll need to drop the shortcut icon right on the Shortcuts or a group header for this to work correctly.

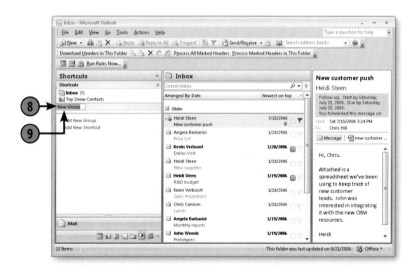

Dragging Items to Create Shortcuts

① Click the Folder button to open the folder list.

② Click on and drag an item to the Shortcuts button, and hold it there without releasing the mouse button.

③ The Shortcuts pane opens.

④ Continue to drag the folder and drop it on the desired shortcut group header.

⑤ Outlook creates a shortcut to the item.

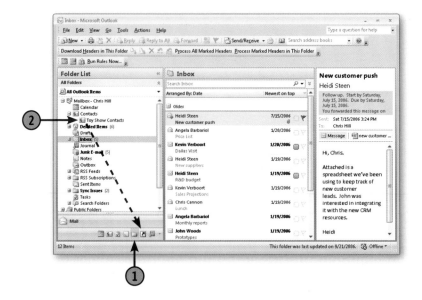

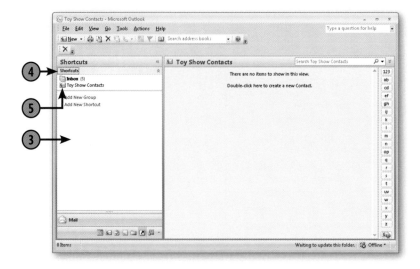

Adding Shortcuts to Non-Outlook Items

① Locate in Windows Explorer a program for which you want to create a shortcut.

② Right-click the program and choose Send To.

③ Click Desktop (Create Shortcut).

④ Windows creates a shortcut on the Windows desktop

⑤ Open Outlook and position it so you can see the shortcut on the desktop.

⑥ Click the Shortcuts button to open the Shortcuts pane.

⑦ Drag the shortcut from the desktop to the target shortcut group header.

⑧ Outlook adds the shortcut to the group.

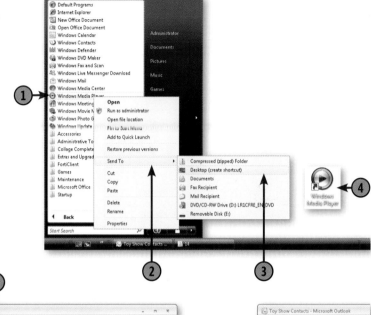

Customizing the Outlook Toolbars

Outlook includes several toolbars that contain dozens of toolbar buttons. Most users, however, use only a handful of toolbar buttons during any given Outlook session. Outlook enables you to add or remove toolbar buttons, and even add or remove an entire toolbar.

Add or Remove a Toolbar

1 Choose Toolbars from the View menu.

2 If a toolbar is displaying, it will have a checkmark next to it. Select the toolbar to hide it.

3 Select a nonchecked toolbar to display it.

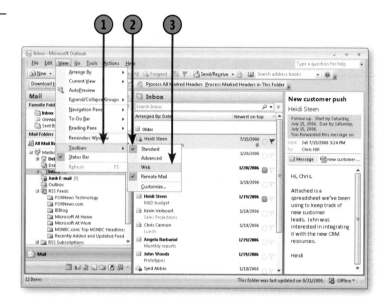

Tip

To quickly toggle toolbars on and off, right-click the toolbar and choose the toolbar's name from the submenu.

Tip

To quickly add or remove a button to a toolbar, click the Toolbar Options arrow at the far-right end of the toolbar. Select Add Or Remove Buttons, and then select the name of the toolbar (such as Standard) you want to edit. You can then add or remove buttons from the list that appears. Be careful, though, too many buttons makes it difficult to find commands.

Caution

Be selective when choosing the number of buttons you add to a toolbar. Unless you use a high screen resolution and have a large monitor, Outlook may not be able to display all the toolbar buttons at once.

Try This!

To move a toolbar, click and hold the vertical dashed bar at its left end and drag it to a different location.

Create a New Toolbar

① Choose Toolbars from the View menu.

② Choose Customize.

③ Click the Toolbars tab.

④ Click New.

⑤ Type a name for the toolbar.

⑥ Click OK.

(continued on the next page)

Tip

To close your new toolbar, click its Close button.

Try This!

Click the down arrow on the new toolbar. Click Add Or Remove Buttons from the submenu. Choose Customize from the next submenu. Add buttons from the Commands tab. Click Close.

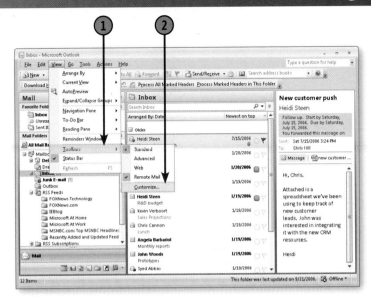

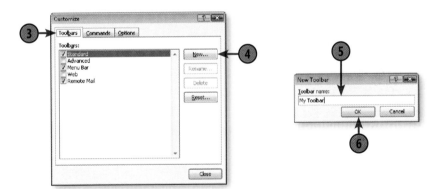

Create a New Toolbar *(continued)*

7 Click the Commands tab.

8 Drag buttons from the Commands list to the blank toolbar.

9 Click Close.

10 If desired, drag the new toolbar and dock it under your other toolbars.

Tip

To rename a toolbar, click the Toolbars tab, select the toolbar you want to rename, and click Rename. Type a new name, and click OK. Outlook only allows you to rename custom toolbars.

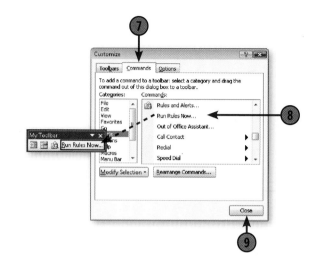

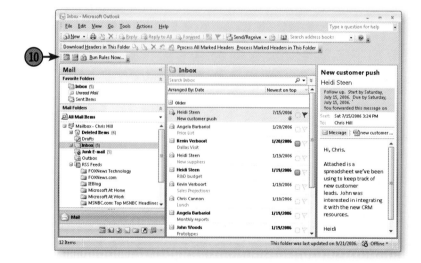

Index

A

Access. *See* Microsoft Office Access
Account Settings dialog box, 39, 96–97, 100, 220, 226, 233
Actions, Categorize, All Categories command, 123
Actions, Create, New Journal Entry command, 196
Actions, Create, New Journal Entry For Contact command, 132
Actions, Create, New Meeting Request To Contact command, 128
Actions, Create, New Message To Contact command, 126
Actions, Forward command, 154, 189
Actions, Junk E-mail command, 86
Actions, New Mail Message Using command, 65
Actions, New Meeting Request command, 143
Actions, Plan A Meeting command, 143
Actions, Send As Business Card command, 131
Actions, Send Full Contact command, 130
Add New Category dialog box, 204
Add New E-Mail Account dialog box, 38–39
Add or Remove buttons command, 247
Add To Outlook Contacts command, 106
Address Book, 47–48, 50–52, 114
Address Book dialog box, 51–52
address cards, 107
Address Cards view, 118–19
Advanced Find command, 121
Advanced Find dialog box, 121

Advanced Options dialog box, 44
All Attendees list, 143
All Categories command, 25
All Outlook Items folder list, 212
all-day events, 141
antivirus program, 81
appointment calendar, printing, 155
appointment form, 140
appointment items, embedding documents, 150
Appointment window, 129, 139
appointments, 16, 139
    adding, 138–41
    categorizing, 140
    changing, 145
    copying, 187
    day, 139
    description of, 139
    extended information about, 139
    lines for, 17
    multiple-day, 139
    opening, 42
    printing, 139
    recurring, 145
    reminders, 152
    sharing information about, 140
    short subjects, 138
    starting time, 139
    subject, 140
    viewing, 20, 137
Archive dialog box, 232
archive files, 3
Archive Folders, 215
archiving
    backing up files, 232
    e-mail, 23

archiving, *continued*
    items, 215
    Outlook data files, 230–32
    selective, 224
articles, downloading, 103
attachments, 67–68, 81–82
    Calendar item, 154, 156
    files and printing, 178
    format of, 68
    forwarding e-mail, 84
    items inserted as, 171
    opening, 81
    previewing, 22
    printing, 115
    replying to e-mail, 83
    saving, 82
    viruses, 81
attendees, 144, 147
AutoArchive dialog box, 230–31
AutoArchive feature, 230–31
AutoDialer feature, 108

B

backing up, 226–27
    archive files, 232
    contacts, 113
    selective, 224
Backup program, 227
blocking
    domains, 87
    people, 103
bold text, 60
Business Cards view, 118
Business phone number, 127

N

Navigation Pane, 8–9
  Add or Remove Buttons option, 194
  Address Cards, 119
  Calendar icon, 16, 239
  Calendar list, 42
  By Category, 188
  collapsing, 28
  Configure Buttons option, 194
  Contacts icon, 108, 113, 115, 119
  customizing, 29, 241–45
  Drafts folder, 71
  Entry List button, 198
  Folder List icon, 122–23, 167, 212
  folders, 32, 34
  hiding, 28, 241
  Inbox icon, 6, 75
  Journal icon, 194
  Mail icon, 71, 76, 208
  Mailbox, 42
  Message tab, 6
  Microsoft Office button, 115
  My Contacts area, 123
  Notes List, 182, 188
  Options tab, 6–7
  Outbox, 70
  Personal Folders, 42
  RSS Feeds folder, 96, 98
  Save & Close icon, 35
  Sent Items folder, 71
  shortcut group, 242–43
  Shortcuts button, 242
  Shortcuts list, 243
  showing, 241
  Simple List, 166
  To-Do List, 159
  views, 43
New All Day Event command, 141

New Call dialog box, 127
New Entry dialog box, 114
New Folder command, 20, 221
New Message window, 49
New Outlook Data File dialog box, 220
New RSS Feed dialog box, 97
New Search Folder command, 208
New Signature dialog box, 63
non-Outlook items shortcuts, 245
Normal command, 10
notes, 181, 186
  copying, 182–84, 191
  printing, 190
  reading, 183
  sharing, 189–91
  viewing, 182–83
  Windows desktop, 184
Notes folder, 3, 35, 181–83, 187–88
Notes List view, 182
notes window, 184

O

Object dialog box, 151
objects and Calendar item, 149–51
Office tools, 3
offline folder file (OST), 219
offline folders, 233–34
Offline Help, 46
Open in New Window command, 108
Options dialog box
  Add Holidays option, 240
  Advanced Options, 44
  AutoArchive option, 230
  Blocked Senders tab, 87
  Calendar Options option, 239–40
  Compose In This Message Format drop-down list, 238
  E-mail Options option, 236

Options dialog box, *continued*
  Empty The Deleted Items Folder Upon Exiting option, 217
  Journal Options option, 199–200
  Junk E-mail, 85
  Mail Format tab, 62, 64, 66, 238
  Mail Setup tab, 70, 74
  Other tab, 44, 217, 230
  Preferences tab, 85, 87, 199–200, 236, 239–40
  Remove button, 87
  Schedule An Automatic Send/Receive Every X Minutes option, 74
  Send Immediately When Connected check box, 70
  Send/Receive, 74
  Signatures, 62, 64
  Stationery And Fonts, 66
Out of Office Assistant, scheduling, 22
Outbox folder, 32, 69, 72
outgoing messages, 32
Outlook 2007 profile and Exchange Server accounts, 220
Outlook Bar, 182–83
Outlook data files, 219
  archiving, 230–32
  backing up, 226–27
  creation, 220–21
  restoring, 228–29
Outlook Data Files dialog box, 221
Outlook Express, 40
Outlook folders, 111
  quick access to, 8–9
  sending message to, 70
  sharing, 163
  viewing size, 215
Outlook icon, 30
Outlook items
  adding to task, 170–71
  categories, 187

About the Author

Jim Boyce has authored and co-authored over 50 books about applications, operating systems, and programming. Jim's best-selling Outlook books have helped thousands of Office users learn to tame Outlook and make the most of its many features. Jim also writes frequently for the Work Essentials area of the Microsoft Office Web site at http://office.microsoft.com. He was a Contributing Editor to *WINDOWS Magazine* as well as a frequent contributor to techrepublic.com and many other online and print publications.

What do you think of this book?

We want to hear from you!

Do you have a few minutes to participate in a brief online survey?

Microsoft is interested in hearing your feedback so we can continually improve our books and learning resources for you.

To participate in our survey, please visit:

www.microsoft.com/learning/booksurvey/

...and enter this book's ISBN-10 number (appears above barcode on back cover*). As a thank-you to survey participants in the United States and Canada, each month we'll randomly select five respondents to win one of five $100 gift certificates from a leading online merchant. At the conclusion of the survey, you can enter the drawing by providing your e-mail address, which will be used for prize notification only.

Thanks in advance for your input. Your opinion counts!

Microsoft
Press

* Where to find the ISBN-10 on back cover

Example only. Each book has unique ISBN.